W9-CDP-075

THE MODERN
CORPORATION

THE MODERN CORPORATION

CORPORATION

Free Markets versus Regulation

Nicholas Wolfson

THE FREE PRESS
A Division of Macmillan, Inc.
NEW YORK

Collier Macmillan Publishers
LONDON

The Free Press
A Division of Macmillan, Inc.
866 Third Avenue, New York, N.Y. 10022

Collier Macmillan Canada, Inc.

Printed in the United States of America

printing number
1 2 3 4 5 6 7 8 9 10

Library of Congress Cataloging in Publication Data

Wolfson, Nicholas.
  The modern corporation.

  Includes index.
  1. Industry and state—United States. 2. Corporation
law—United States. 3. Corporations—United States.
I. Title.
HD3616.U47W57 1984   338.7′4′0973   84-13645
ISBN 0-02-934700-9

Acknowledgments

   The author wishes to thank the copyright holders of the following works who permitted in-
clusions of quotations in this book:
Adolph A. Berle, Jr., and Gardiner C. Means, *The Modern Corporation and Private Property* (1932,
   1960). Copyright © 1932, 1960 by Macmillan Publishing Company.
"Vertical Integration, Appropriable Rents and the Competitive Contracting Process," by
   B. Klein, R. Crawford, and A. Alchian, *Journal of Law and Economics* 21 (1978):297. Copyright
   © 1978 by the University of Chicago, all rights reserved.
T. Easterbrook and D. Fischel, "The Proper Role of a Target's Management in Responding to a
   Tender Offer," *Harvard Law Review* 94 (1981): 1161. Copyright © 1981 by the Harvard Law
   Review Association.
Michael C. Jensen, "Corporate Control: Folklore vs Science," *Managerial Economics Research Cen-
   ter* Working Paper No. MERC 83-07 (University of Rochester, Rochester, N.Y., March 1983).
G. Stigler and C. Friedland, "The Literature of Economics: The Case of Berle and Means,"
   Journal of Law and Economics 26 (1983): 237. Copyright © (1983) by the University of Chicago, all
   rights reserved.
H. Demsetz, "The Structure of Ownership and the Theory of the Firm," *Journal of Law and Eco-
   nomics* 26 (1983): 375. Copyright © 1983 by the University of Chicago, all rights reserved.
Statement of the Business Roundtable on the American Law Institute's "Proposed Principles of
   Corporate Governance and Structure: Restatement and Recommendations" (February 1983).

A. Ehrbar, "Index Funds-An Idea Whose Time Has Come," *Fortune,* June 1976.

J. Langbein and R. Posner, "Market Funds and Trust-Investment Law," *American Bar Foundation Research Journal* 1 (1976).

The following articles by Nicholas Wolfson with changes have been utilized in portions of this book with permission of the copyright holders:

N. Wolfson, "A Critique of the Securities and Exchange Commission," *Emory Law Journal* 30 (1981): 119. Copyright © by N. Wolfson 1981, reprinted by permission of the *Emory Law Journal,* Emory University School of Law, Atlanta, Georgia 30322.

N. Wolfson, "SEC Thinking About Corporate Governance and Accountability: Lessons in Bureaucratizing the Entrepreneurial Corporation," in *Corporate Governance: Past and Future* (1982). Copyright © 1982 by KCG Productions, Inc.

N. Wolfson, "A Critique of Corporate Law," *University of Miami Law Review* 34 (1980): 959. Copyright © 1980 by the *Review.*

N. Wolfson, "Securities Regulation, New Theories of Portfolio Management Challenge SEC Doctrine," *The Corporation Law Review,* Vol. 1, No. 1 (Winter 1978). Copyright © 1978 by Warren, Gorham & Lamont, Inc., 210 South Street, Boston, Mass., all rights reserved.

N. Wolfson, "Securities Regulation, Two Cheers for Regulation D," *The Corporation Law Review,* Vol. 6, No. 1 (Winter 1983). Copyright © 1983 by Warren, Gorham & Lamont, Inc., 210 South Street, Boston, Mass., all rights reserved.

N. Wolfson, "The Market for Public Accounting Services: Demand, Supply and Regulation, A Commentary," by Nicholas Wolfson, Vol. II, No. 1 (Winter 1979–80), reprinted by permission of *The Accounting Journal.*

N. Wolfson, "The Need for Empirical Research in Securities Law," *Southern California Law Review* 49 (1976): 286. Reprinted with the permission of the *Southern California Law Review.*

N. Wolfson, book review of Neil Jacoby's "Corporate Power and Social Responsibility," *Connecticut Law Review* 6 (Winter 1973–1974): 360. Reprinted by permission of the *Law Review* and Fred B. Rothman & Co.

To Judith

Contents

Preface _____

THE LEGITIMACY AND TRUE CHARACTER of the large publicly held corporation have been for too long a time gravely misunderstood by the experts and the general public. The large corporation is an enormously important component of the American free enterprise society. The failure to understand its nature, therefore, can prove fatal to an informed acceptance of the value of the American corporation. Efforts to unduly regulate it can undermine its efficiency. In this book I set out to establish a proper basis for the legitimacy of the American corporation and its management. That effort requires a critique of state legal concepts as well as a reevaluation of the worth of the Securities and Exchange Commission, the primary federal regulator of the large corporation.

Portions of this book are based on prior articles. The materials in those pieces, however, have been extensively redone, restructured, and made current.

I would like to acknowledge the research assistance of Bridget Jenkins while a student at the University of Connecticut School of Law.

PART I

Traditional Theory

1

Overview of Traditional Corporate Law

CORPORATE LAW IN the United States is based upon the assumption that the modern large publicly held corporation is a powerful ministate run by control groups that need legal checks and balances.[1] The principal object of corporate law, therefore, is an attempt to articulate a constitution designed to define and limit the powers and prerogatives of the centers of corporate power: the senior management and the board of directors.[2] In eager pursuit of that objective, attorneys and judges have vigorously expanded the scope and complexity of corporate law. Consequently, power in the corporation has increasingly moved out of the executive suites into law offices and the courts. Since the corporation is not a ministate, however, but a dynamic competitive economic entity circumscribed by powerful free-market forces, the law has been built upon a false assumption. As is always the case when fiction overwhelms fact in the law, the shape of corporate law has evolved into a twisted and contorted configuration. The general and specific theories underlying corporate legal concepts thus have for generations floated in mid-air free from any mooring in empirical data or sound economic philosophy. This book will endeavor to correct these false assumptions and create a rigorous theory of the corporation. In doing so it will develop and apply modern economic theories of the firm to the corporation and demonstrate that

3

the publicly held corporation is a natural product of the enlightened preferences of shareholders and positively benefits the general public. It will demonstrate the value of free-market constraints on corporate management and the inefficiencies and weaknesses of state and federal regulation of the publicly held corporation.

Two kinds of corporation must be distinguished: the closely held and the publicly held. The former is characterized by a relatively small number of shareholders, perhaps one, two, several, or a few score. This small body of owners frequently shares in the operation of the business; that is, one group both owns and controls the business. Since the shareholders are few in number and the business is usually quite small and unknown to the general public, there is no active market for the purchase and sale of the shares of stock held by the owners. Although some closely held corporations are gigantic (only a few decades ago Ford Motor Corporation was closely held by the Ford family), most are of small to medium size. The corporate firms that dominate the economic structure of the United States, however, are the publicly held corporations. Their shareholders may number in the thousands or the hundreds of thousands. These organizations form the subject of this book. They include corporate giants such as AT&T and General Motors, as well as other corporations that are large, but not as large as the one hundred or so titans that dominate the business landscape. In those corporations the shareholders are usually passive stakeholders who do not take part in any sense in the management of the corporation. Hence the expression made popular by the Berle and Means book, *The Modern Corporation and Private Property:* "separation of ownership from control."[3] This "separation" phenomenon has become the traditional mode of picturing the fundamental problem of corporate law and economics. The small group of managers are considered to be relatively free to manage the publicly held corporations for their own benefit, not that of the powerless and passive public shareholders.

The student of the corporation thus confronts two separate entities: the world of the closely held corporation and the universe of the publicly held corporation. It is with respect to the publicly held corporation that the legal rules are expected to protect the welfare of hundreds of thousands of shareholders. The great problems of corporate law and economics—issues of size and power, and social and environmental impact and control—are those of the publicly held corporation. This book will attempt to correct persistent and popular errors in corporate law and economics and develop a modern and systematic theory of the corporation.

State law governs the shape and content of corporate rights and obligations. In each of the fifty states a corporate statute articulates the structure of corporate form and the obligations and rights of the officers, shareholders, and directors who constitute the dramatis personae of the corporate stage.[4] In the popular and conventional mode the corporation is pictured as a pyramid. At the base are the shareholders who have contributed the risk capital for the enterprise. Their personal liability is limited by statute to the amount they have invested, hence the well-known expression "limited liability." They are assumed to be the owners of the enterprise and as such have rights to share in profits when distributed and have the power to elect annually the supreme governing body, the board of directors. Further, they must approve by prescribed voting percentages certain defined organic changes in the structure of the entity. All of this and more seems right and obvious since they are considered to be the owners of the business and therefore the ultimate sovereigns of the assumed corporate ministate. Accordingly, if you peruse typical state statutes you will find numerous provisions which condition certain kinds of fundamental corporate actions such as mergers and sale of all the assets upon majority or two-thirds vote of the shareholders.[5] The shareholder vote, however, is not of the "one person, one vote" variety. Shareholders enjoy one vote for each share they hold. The important investor with thirty thousand shares has thirty thousand votes; the small investor with one share has one vote.

The body with plenary authority over the operations of the business is designated the board of directors by state statutes.[6] The directors have the legal power to determine the location of major plants, the amount and timing of major borrowings, mix of products, price of new equity—in short, the entire range and direction of the business and financial life of the corporation. Just as traditional scholarship makes the analogy between the shareholders in corporation law and the sovereign voters of a state, so traditional corporate scholars analogize the directors to the governor, or perhaps to a combination of governor and legislators, whom the voters elect. Under state law certain important corporate actions require board or board plus shareholder approval. Other actions require only board action. The board of directors under state law elect the principal officers of the corporation such as the president, vice-president, and chairman of the board. These individuals, constituting senior management, administer the business affairs of the corporation. They plan the building of factories, hire middle management, and in general have the authority as granted to them by the directors to decide the thousands of issues that arise in the running of the modern corporation.

In legal theory the corporate business is managed by senior officers under the ultimate direction of the board of directors, who have the responsibility and power to establish the guidelines to be followed by the senior management group. There is some debate today whether boards in any sense directly manage the business or merely passively monitor the actions of the senior management. Most commentators conclude that in many cases, if not most, senior management and not the board are in reality the dominant force in the corporation.[7]

The state statutes we have referred to are in part a lengthy check list of powers and responsibilities of the officers, directors, and shareholders. A corporation through its officers may consider the sale of all of its assets to another corporation. Who can authorize that action? The typical state statute will require approval of both the board and the shareholders by specified votes. The statute will deny that power to the officers. A corporation may consider merger with another corporation. The usual state statute will require approval of both the board and the shareholders. Again a corporation may consider closing down a plant in Connecticut and moving the operation to Georgia. Case law in conjunction with statute may indicate that senior management alone has the power to make this decision. The traditional mode of operation in that corporation may dictate that such an important decision be put before the board of directors even though the officers have the technical authority to proceed alone. Attorneys may even recommend submission of the decision to the shareholders at a special meeting in order to lessen the possibility of a successful shareholder suit for violation of certain duties of management and directors. This will be discussed subsequently in Chapters 6 and 7.

The state statutes are also preoccupied with matters such as technical rules for obtaining the proper quorum for shareholder and director meetings, specification of various voting percentages for different actions, and the like. Additional material dealt with by the statutes govern such matters as the place of meetings, notice and waiver requirements for meetings, and the kinds of documents that must be filed with state authorities when various actions are taken.

Two fundamental concepts in corporate law are the notions of duty of loyalty[8] and duty of care.[9] The latter typically requires a director or senior manager to perform his duties in "good faith" in a manner he "reasonably believes" to be in the "best interests of the corporation" and with such care "as an ordinarily prudent person in like position would use under similar circumstances."[10] This is essentially a kind of ill-defined competency obligation. Although directors are not required to guarantee corporate success, and are permitted to make mistakes, at some ill-defined point a director's nonattention, negligent attention, or grossly negligent attention to data, or his negligent or grossly negligent exercise of judgment will subject him to a successful shareholder suit where damages can be proven. The reference in the test above to "good faith" means that the director must honestly endeavor to fulfill his requirement of competency. The reference to "ordinarily prudent person in like position" employs a customary legal method similar to the reasonable man test in other areas. The court is expected to use that standard in a case-by-case analysis of proper behavior.

It is at once apparent that the courts can fill the vaguely defined concepts in a harsh or a liberal mode. The purpose is to establish some minimum level of directorial and senior-management competency for the benefit of the shareholders. In subsequent chapters we will analyze the lack of connection between the goal and the means to achieve it. Suffice to say at this point that the courts establish varying verbal standards without any scientifically organized methods of establishing an empirical connection between the standard and the results in the real world of management behavior. The current dispute in the courts and the law reviews centers on conflicting verbal formulations.[11] Some courts and commentators would restrict successful shareholder suits to those cases where the directors or senior management can be proven to have made "off the wall" decisions that have little or no rational explanation. Other courts would apply what they term an objective test in which they explicate a standard against which competency is measured. The latter criterion means in effect that the judges substitute their own business judgment for that of the directors in the given case.

The term "business judgment" is the pervasive phrase used in all the cases. In effect the courts assert that a director will have fulfilled his duty of care to shareholders and corporation if he uses business judgment. The legal formula further asserts that judges will not second-guess directors' business judgments unless made in bad faith (e.g., in return for a bribe). As explained above, however, some courts will be more willing to second-guess the judgment than others. For example, assume that a corporation determines to build a large plant in Hartford, Connecticut. Minority shareholders attack the decision in court on the ground that the construction and operation of the plant would have been far more inexpensive in neighboring Massachusetts. The court will be quick to dismiss the suit on the authority of the business judgment rule. Suppose, however, that plaintiffs introduce cogent evidence that the board of directors and senior management did not examine engineering reports or any other cost studies, all of which indicated the superiority of the Massachusetts location. The court might then award the action to plaintiffs on the grounds that no business judgment was exercised. Now assume that defendants introduce evidence that a small minority of the engineering and cost reports indicated the superiority of Connecticut and that the directors were familiar with all the reports. Plaintiffs might still succeed if the courts develop an objective duty of care doctrine that requires the directors to make only "reasonable" judgments, such as judgments based on the majority opinion in the reports. In jurisdictions allowing greater room for directorial error and mistake or discretion, defendants will prevail on the ground that courts will not reverse directorial business judgment even if they think it is wrong so long as it was honestly and with some degree of care decided. Attorneys advise and charge fees based upon their knowledge of the subtleties of the differing jurisdictions and the nuances of the varying legal doctrines. All the courts pay deference to the notion that people in business must be free within reasonable limits to take the usual amount of risk entailed in the operation of essentially risky ventures and that courts are not as well equipped as businesspeople to make those decisions. However, as we have mentioned, the degree to which one verbal formulation of the test as compared to another appropriately "liberates" or "unduly" shackles directors is totally unknown.

There is a companion legal doctrine that is of even greater significance in the scheme of things: the duty of loyalty. This is a principle borrowed from trust law that transforms directors and senior management into trustees, for all the shareholders, who must always subordinate their own self-interest to that of all the shareholders.[12] It is a kind of ethical principle that comes into operation in every transaction where the directors or management have a self-interest or conflict of interest and at the same time render a decision that affects the shareholders. In those cases the test is not the relatively liberal business judgment rule but the test of fairness. For example, if the directors in the case of the Connecticut plant location referred to above are financially interested in the Connecticut land site that is to be sold to the corporation, then the duty of loyalty as well as the duty of care comes into operation. In virtually all of the jurisdictions in the United States the board of directors will have to demonstrate that despite their self-interest in, for example, a Connecticut rather than Massachusetts location, the decision was fair to the corporation. Fair in this context means that disinterested directors would have decided to build in Connecticut. At this juncture it should be clear that the court is now into the second-guessing game with a vengeance. The defendants will have to convince a court that the decision was "wise," indeed "correct," not that it was a more or less rational decision, albeit wrong. In effect the judges must determine what they as directors with no conflict of interest would have decided to do. Of course other related judicial doctrines are at work in this area. The defendants will frequently have a greater chance of success if they consult in advance of the decision with a group of disinterested directors and construction experts. Even better, if they put the decision to build in Connecticut first to those on the board who have no financial interest in the construction, and in addition place the decision up for vote by shareholders, then the procedural fairness of the situation will improve their chances in court.[13] This would probably be true even if management had full control over the proxy or voting machinery and great influence and complete rapport with their disinterested colleagues on the board.

As is apparent, the directors' business judgment rule is always subject to the tougher duty of a loyalty test where the directors' decision is potentially clouded by the existence or appearance of conflict of interest. Most litigation involves plaintiffs' efforts to introduce a duty of loyalty attack rather than a simple duty of care attack that is less likely to succeed.[14] However, to the extent that courts begin to toughen the tests of duty of care and business judgment they begin to approach the nature and extent of the duty of loyalty test.

An enormous amount of legal time and skill is expended in either avoiding or introducing duty of loyalty litigation. Every major management or directorial decision is potentially subject to an attack of unfairness. In every merger between two corporations there is always the expectation that a group of minority shareholders will retain expensive counsel to attack the transaction on the grounds that it was not fair to X class of shareholders. Every significant purchase or sale of assets is potentially subject to the same attack. In like manner, management compensation arrangements, plant selection, and changes in control are exposed to a searching fairness test in the courts.

Corporation law has become a kind of judicial mode of applied ethics in which every significant management decision is subject to a fairness inquiry. Notwithstanding the frequency of these inquiries, the judiciary has not proven any more successful than any other group in society or in other areas establishing an acceptable test of fairness. The fairness test, after all, frequently comes into play in these fuzzy areas where the criminal law does not apply. In those situations where a director or officer commits theft, larceny, or embezzlement the criminal law applies—as it does to all of us. The duty of loyalty test is introduced into these areas where the criminal law has not necessarily been violated. In typical duty of loyalty cases the courts determine fairness on a case-by-case basis that defies any organizing principle. It is impossible to use the prior cases to make predictions of future results. The courts write opinions and determine results based upon a visceral reaction and rhetorical references to fairness. The defense for this is the principle underlying all corporate law: publicly held corporations operate in noncompetitive markets with no major constraints on management except that which can be provided by law.

What we have described up to here is under the domain of state statutes and state judicial decisions. The second major area of traditional corporate law is securities regulation. The first piece of federal securities legislation enacted by the U.S. Congress was the Securities Act of 1933.[15] This so-called truth-in-disclosure law requires corporations to make detailed and voluminous business and financial disclosures in connection with the public sale of securities. Corporations must file a registration statement with the Securities and Exchange Commission (SEC) describing the strengths and weaknesses of the business and are required to distribute the registration statement, or more precisely a portion of it called the prospectus, to prospective buyers. If the corporate seller of securities makes a material misstatement or omits material statements necessary for a complete picture, purchasers may sue the corporation, directors, and senior management for damages. The purpose of the legislation was to change the legal doctrine from "buyer beware" to "seller beware." The Securities Exchange Act of 1934 prohibits omissions and misrepresentations of material facts in connection with any purchase or sale of securities in interstate commerce or by use of the mails; it also subjects the continuous trading in securities that takes place on the exchanges and in over-the-counter markets to SEC and judicial oversight.[16] The 1934 Act also requires publicly held corporations, whose stock is traded on exchanges or that exceed certain size parameters to supply on a continuous basis financial and business information to the public. In the years since the passage of these two acts, the Securities and Exchange Commission has created a complex regulatory system of mandatory disclosure that forces publicly held corporations to generate frequent and enormously lengthy and detailed disclosure documents. The regulatory apparatus has brought in its wake full employment for a legion of public accountants and attorneys to help interpret and enforce the legislation. Until about a decade ago there was a consensus that the federal system of mandatory disclosure was a valuable vehicle for investor protection. In the past ten years a wealth of new economic and empirical studies have cast doubt upon the value of the system, and have even documented serious distortions in the disclosure system caused by SEC regulation.[17] These are all matters that will be developed in detail in later sections of this work.

These few pages obviously constitute a first impression or mini-course in modern corporate law. The crucial point which bears repeating is that the law first assumes that the publicly held large corporation is a kind of government free from the discipline of a free competitive market. The purpose of constitutional law is to protect the voters from overreaching government; likewise, the purpose of corporate law is to guard apparently helpless shareholders from the self-interest, cupidity, and incompetence of management directors. Hence the doctrines of duty of care and duty of loyalty and SEC mandatory disclosure.

Two questions inevitably arise: First, is the system working effectively to accomplish its goals? Second, are there superior methods to accomplish the goals? In order to answer those questions we will have to explore the economic reality of the corporate structure and the capital markets in which it exists.

2

Berle and Means's
Theory of the Corporation

CORPORATE AND SECURITIES LAW regulates directors and management of publicly held corporations. The justification and rationale for regulation is based upon the notion of the separation of ownership by passive shareholders from that of control by a small self-perpetuating management group. The growth of this phenomenon and the supposed divergence of interest between ownership and control received its classic exposition in the brilliant and famous work *The Modern Corporation and Private Property* by Adolf A. Berle, Jr., and Gardner C. Means, published in 1932. The authors examined the nature of control exercised over the 200 largest American corporations at the beginning of the 1930s. They concluded that "65 percent of the companies and 80 percent of their combined wealth"[1] were controlled by the management or by a legal device (e.g., voting trusts or nonvoting stock) involving a small proportion of ownership. They cited some examples now very familiar:

> The stockholder lists of the largest railroad, the Pennsylvania Railroad, the largest public utility, the American Telephone and Telegraph Company, and the largest industrial, the United States Steel Corporation, show in each case that the principal holder in 1929 owned less than one percent of the outstanding stock.[2]

Since no one individual or group owned a controlling block in such corporations, Berle and Means demonstrated that control over the operations of the giant companies had lodged in the small group of directors and senior management that ran the corporation from day to day. They exercised their dominion over the proxy machinery to reelect themselves year after year. As Berle and Means pointed out,

> In the election of the board the stockholder ordinarily has three alternatives. He can refrain from voting, he can attend the annual meeting and personally vote his stock, or he can sign a proxy transferring his voting power to certain individuals selected by the management of the corporation, the proxy committee. As his personal vote will count for little or nothing at the meeting unless he has a large block of stock, the stockholder is practically reduced to the alternative of not voting at all or else of *handing over his vote to individuals over whom he has no control and in whose selection he did not participate.*[3]

Since incumbent management decides whom the proxy committee will vote for they "virtually dictate their own successors."[4] Even if state law or corporate charter requires a sizable quorum for an annual meeting, incumbent management has no problem in getting it through its ability to solicit tens of thousands of proxies by mail or personal contact at corporate expense. Although outside groups of shareholders may nominate their own slate of directorial nominees and campaign for shareholder votes or proxies, the process is so expensive that only extremely wealthy groups can finance the effort. The cost of mailing proxy solicitation materials alone to hundreds of thousands of shareholders costs a great amount. When to this is added the cost of the inevitable legal battles, printing fees for the solicitation materials, costs of retaining accountants, and financial advisers, the aggregate costs are now, and were even in Berle and Means's time, immense. Incumbent management under traditional legal doctrine do not pay these expenses; they are borne by the corporate treasury. Berle and Means concluded:

> For the most part the stockholder is able to play only the part of the rubber stamp. . . the usual stockholder has little power. . . . The separation of ownership and control has become virtually complete. The bulk of the owners have in fact almost no control over the enterprise, while those in control hold only a negligible proportion of the total ownership.[5]

Berle and Means pointed out that the shareholders hope and expect that management will earn the ''maximum profit compatible with a reasonable degree of risk.''[6] Will management seek that same end or some other goal at odds with the interest of shareholders? The authors concluded that if management's prime motivating force is the ''desire for *personal profit*''[7] then the divergence of interest between the two groups will be complete. Even control groups with a relatively large stock interest will profit by diverting income from the corporation: ''If such persons can make a profit of a million dollars from a sale of property to the corporation, they can afford to suffer a loss of $600,000 through the ownership of 60 percent of the stock, since the transaction will still net them $400,000. . . .''[8] If management is prompted by other motives, Berle and Means are uncertain of the result. For example ''the interests of owner and control may run parallel, as when control seeks the prestige of 'success' and profits for the controlled enterprise [are] the current measure of success.''[9] Throughout the book, however, the authors clearly expect serious divergence in fact; indeed the authors elsewhere liken the corporate system to the communist system:

> It is an odd paradox that a corporate board of directors and a communist committee of commisars should so nearly meet in a common contention. The communist thinks of the community in terms of a state; the corporation director thinks of it in terms of an enterprise; and though this difference between the two may well lead to a radical divergence in results, it still remains true that the corporation director who would subordinate the interests of the individual stockholder to those of the group more nearly resembles the communist in mode of thought than he does the protagonist of private propery.[10]

Berle and Means contrast the publicly held corporation to the classic Adam Smith enterprise in which the owner managed as well as owned the business. ''By carrying on enterprise he would employ his energy and wealth in such a way as to obtain more wealth. In this effort he would tend to make for profit those things which were in most demand.''[11] First, the owner of the small enterprise is spurred on by the expectation of profits to risk his wealth. Second, the drive to maximize his investment by making profits spurs the owner-manager of the firm to use his greatest skill and effort to maximize efficiency. Efficiency in this sense is simply the ability to satisfy the wants of consumers. In the case of

the publicly held corporation the shareholders still hope to maximize profits and hence the value of their risk capital. The control
group, however, may seek to maximize salaries and the good and
easy executive life—large executive suites, beautiful secretaries,
hunting lodges, and expensive paintings on the office wall. As
Adam Smith himself wrote:

> The directors of such companies . . . [he was talking about joint
> stock companies, the eighteenth century equivalent of the corpora-
> tion] being the managers rather of other people's money than of
> their own, it cannot well be expected that they should watch over it
> with the same anxious vigilance with which the partners in a private
> copartnery frequently watch over their own. Like the stewards of a
> rich man, they are apt to consider attention to small matters as not
> for their master's honor, and very easily give themselves a dispensa-
> tion from having it. Negligence and profusion, therefore, must
> always prevail, more or less, in the management of the affairs of
> such a company.[12]

Berle and Means emphasized that the modern corporation is
"so different from the small, privately owned enterprise of the
past as to make the concept of private enterprise an ineffective instrument of analysis."[13] Adam Smith could accurately describe
the drive for personal profit as an effective and socially beneficent
mechanism, but Berle and Means argued that this cannot work in
the modern corporation because of the divergence of interest between control and ownership. They concluded that modern corporations, unlike the smaller units of Adam Smith's day, operate
in noncompetitive markets "dominated by a few great enterprises"[14] in which individual initiative has disappeared. "Group
activity . . . necessarily implies . . . the acceptance of authority
almost to the point of autocracy."[15]

In the opinion of Berle and Means, the law's response to this
development was the creation of the legal obligations of duty and
care referred to in the first chapter. But the legal effort has not
been successful because the courts ultimately lack the "ability to
handle the problems involved."[16] The power of control to divert
profits and assets to its own benefit—to feather its nest at the expense of shareholders—is too great for the imperfect mechanisms
of the law to master. This is not to say that the doctrines of corporate law are of no help to shareholders; they are better off with
them than without. In the final analysis, however, Berle and

Means conclude that the shareholders have such an attenuated relationship to the modern corporation that they have surrendered the right to have the corporation operated for their sole benefit. On the other hand, the senior management and other control groups have so little invested in the corporation that they too have no claim to the corporation. Both groups have "rather, cleared the way . . . [for the community to] demand that the modern corporation serve . . . all society."[17] Control must become a "neutral technocracy"[18] that balances the claims of the various interest groups in society and awards to each a portion of the gains on the basis of the public interest rather than private self-interest.

The absolutely crucial element in the Berle and Means analysis is that the divergence of interest between ownership and control is married to the supposedly unbridled discretionary power of directors and management to run the corporation as a private satrapy. It was this combination of elements that Berle and Means believed sundered the connection between the profit motive of the Adam Smith firm and beneficial consequence. The profit motive drove the competitive entrepreneur to seek to satisfy consumer demand. Such efforts will result in proper allocation of resources in the sense that consumer demand will determine the number of firms necessary to satisfy the greatest number of consumers. To the extent that control slacks off in a drive for the easy or the good life rather than the arduous pursuit of profits, this connection between the entrepreneur and the efficient allocation of resources is ended.

With this in mind the modern reader searches the Berle and Means classic for evidence of the systematic divergence of interest between ownership and control. Organized empirical research would have been most welcome; in the year 1932, even significant albeit anecdotal evidence of the misuse of control power would have aided the case. It is rather startling to find out that except for one or two brief references to corporate skullduggery, the book is absolutely bereft of any shred of evidence, anecdotal or otherwise, of the actual divergence of interest. Instead, the book, after development of data demonstrating the dispersion of stock ownership into many small shareholders, devotes over a hundred pages to a demonstration that could not have been new even in 1932 that corporate directors and management have the potential power under the case and statutory law to dominate the financial and business affairs of the corporation. Even that demonstration is purely theoretical in that it refers only to statutory and occasional case law rather than any organized empirical data. None of the Berle and Means discussion, with the literal exception of one or two isolated anecdotal examples, ever proves that free-market forces do not discipline management or that control systematically uses its power to *harm* shareholders or the public.

Ironically the legal developments mentioned again and again throughout the book to ''prove'' the case revolve around the unimportant notions of par and nonpar stock. Berle and Means lamented the passage of statutes permitting the issuance of nonpar stock since they granted to directors the opportunity to ''dilute at will.''[19] In other words, directors could sell stock to one group of investors at $10 per share and a few years later sell the same class of stock to another group at, say, $5 per share, thus diluting the interest of the earlier group. They likewise lamented the development of low-par stock which permitted the same dilution. A high par, say $100, would require a capital contribution to be at least $100. A low par of $5 would permit a later group to pay only $5 per share although the first group of investors paid in, let us say, $100 per share. With the advent of the lower par, Berle and Means complained, the situation in which asset value per share exceeded par became more common and dilution more possible:

> Where the asset value of each share . . . . is $1000 and its par value is $100, it is an obvious dilution of the outstanding shares to issue new shares at $100. . . . As it has become customary to reduce par values, so that the situation in which asset value exceeds par value has become increasingly familiar, this power of dilution at times appears to be really drastic.[20]

It is on the basis of such examples that Berle and Means speculated about the potential for abuse of power by control. As we know today, and financiers probably sensed even in the 1930s, the notions of dilution and concern about low-par or no-par stock expressed by Berle and Means are without foundation. The securities markets are efficient markets (a subject dealt with in detail in later chapters) and the price of a security represents the public's evaluation of the present worth of the business. Although the historic cost of a share may be 1000 dollars per share, if the market price today on an exchange is 100 dollars, that is the true market value of the business today. The original investors who paid in 1000 dollars obviously cannot hope to get investors to pay 1000 dollars today; 100 dollars is all they can get and should get. This is so obvious it hardly bears repeating. Yet on examples such as this and others was made the great case for the suspect nature of the publicly held corporation.

Berle and Means devoted two chapters to the state of corporate financial and business disclosure in pre-SEC days. Although they found serious gaps and omissions in the theoretical structure of the law, they cited no empirical organized data or even significant anecdotal evidence demonstrating deceit or cupidity. Indeed they concluded (although without proof, as usual), "in general, it is the opinion of the writers, that statements contained in brokers' circulars [today called prospectuses] are generally the truth."[21] The authors proceeded to caution that "it is by no means so clear that they are the whole truth and the thing not stated may be far more important than the thing stated,"[22] thus presaging the kind of desire for perfection that the SEC shows in modern times. They pointed out, however, that the law has developed a recission action in which "the far more difficult situation where there has been failure to disclose a fact material to the situation, affords ground for relief."[23] Berle and Means conceded that the offering circular where a New York Stock Exchange (NYSE) listing was involved required "a most elaborate and painstaking disclosure of the material facts in connection with the corporation, which is subjected to a searching analysis by the [exchange listing] committee."[24] The NYSE, asserted the authors, had the "distinct aim" to "provide the market with sufficient information" to permit "appraisal of the security."[25] Further the authors asserted with reference to post fluctuation disclosure that "the banker who has floated an issue of bonds or notes, commonly assures to himself, in his arrangements with a corporation, the right to a continuous flow of information; and a reputable banker will make this information available to the market. . . ."[26] The authors further pointed out that "the New York Stock Exchange . . . insists on periodic statements; and these requirements largely account for the continuous flow of information. . . ."[27] Berle and Means argued that the common law will ultimately hold that "the management of a corporation will be liable (a) for willful misstatement of fact designed to induce action on the part of anyone buying or selling in the market; (b) perhaps also on account of a negligent misstatement of fact not designed to induce action in the market but resulting in a material fluctuation. . . ."[28]

In later chapters we will describe the research of modern economists which demonstrates the extent of voluntary disclosure in pre-SEC days and the proof that SEC statutory disclosure did not improve matters. Suffice it to say that the classic work on the public corporation which spurred on the modern traditional thinking about the corporation established absolutely no empirical or even anecdotal case for deficient disclosure and indeed established that a considerable body of case law (albeit criticized by Berle and Means for many gaps) existed to protect the purchaser and that law was in a process where it might have evolved into even more sophistication in the absence of SEC legislation.

Berle and Means included a section on public stock markets in their study. They emphasized that the state of economic knowledge at the time was in its infancy with respect to the function and operations of the markets.

In a particularly prescient mood they concluded:

> The various incidental rights—voting, preemptive rights . . . and the like, discussed in this Book, all affect and enter into this open market appraisal. *Save as they are likely to do so, they are of little interest to the investor. Economically, the various so-called "legal rights" or the economic pressures which may lead a management to do well by its stockholders, in and of themselves are merely uncertain expectations in the hands of the individual. Aggregated, interpreted by a public market, and appraised in a security exchange,* they do have a *concrete and measurable value;* and it is to this value that the shareholder must and in fact does address himself . . . *in a large measure the corporate security system is based on it.* [Emphasis added.][29]

In addition, they pointed out that the shareholder

> has, in effect, exchanged *control for liquidity.* [Emphasis added.][30]

In these passages Berle and Means almost unknowingly grasped the crucial truth that modern securities markets provide the key to investor protection. The times were too early, the state of economic knowledge too incomplete for them to follow up on the truth. This book, which examined how the efficient securities markets in conjunction with modern notions of the firm protect both the public and the shareholders, could well be summarized by that passage.

In the context of their day the authors reached the conclusion that the modern corporation was an economic state. The law of corporations was in reality a branch of constitutional law for the "new economic state."[31] A new corporate constitutional law and government officials rather than the free market would be used to force the corporation to serve not only the shareholders but also that elusive abstraction called "society."[32] Modern scholarship and federal legislation have attempted to heed that message. It is fair to say that all of modern corporate and SEC learning are based on Berle and Means's vision of the corporation. This book will demonstrate the fundamental flaws in that vision.

3

Reform Movements in Corporate Law After Berle and Means

THE "SEPARATION" THESIS OF Berle and Means has had an enormous impact on the path and pattern of modern corporate and securities law. Reformers through the years have grasped the corpus of traditional corporate law described in Chapter 1 and have attempted to move it into new directions or to infuse it with new vigor in a constant effort to increase the legal constraints upon senior management and other control groups within the corporation. The efforts can be characterized as falling into divergent camps: (1) the traditional liberal reformers, many surprisingly in the ranks of business, but principally academic corporate law professors and the bureaucracy of the Securities and Exchange Commission;[1] and (2) the more radical thinkers, such as Ralph Nader and John Kenneth Galbraith.[2] The traditional reformers have by and large assumed that corporations are not sufficiently responsible to shareholders and have therefore concentrated on using the law to attempt to make directors and management more responsive to them. The more radical reformers have assumed that corporations do not maximize proper resource use or meet consumer demands and have attempted to use the law to make corporations responsive to the community outside the corporation. Both groups, needless to say, have no faith in the operations of the free market to accomplish these goals. Neither group has the support of the shareholder community which is basically content with the protection of the marketplace. The radicals have a profound lack of faith in the legitimacy of the modern corporation and would move government deeper and deeper into the governance of corporations. The traditional reformers share that distrust but with markedly less passion.

TRADITIONAL REFORMERS

The traditional reformers have focused their efforts on the following areas: SEC disclosure, independent directors, a strong directorial committee system, legal devices to increase shareholder democracy, and federal efforts to strengthen duty of care and loyalty concepts.

Corporate state statutes place plenary power over the corporation in the institution of the board of directors. State legislation provides that corporations shall be managed by or under the direction of the board. In recent years research, most notably by Mace, has demonstrated that senior management—in particular one individual, the chief executive officer, frequently the person with the title of president—effectively dominates the affairs of the corporation.[3] Nonmanagement directors, commonly called outside directors, have little voice in management decisions.[4] They act as window dressing, sources of information, and valuable contacts. In occasional emergency situations, as when the chief executive officer (CEO) passes away or is implicated in scandal, they have an important voice in selecting his successor.

Since management determines the composition of the board through its control over the proxy machinery, and since management places itself on the board, there is an apparent built-in conflict of interest: management is able to judge itself. The Securities and Exchange Commission and academic critics in the legal profession believe this conflict is at the root of the separation of ownership and control problem. The solution that has been vigorously pushed is development of the powers of the outside or independent directors and a redefinition of the role of the board.[5]

To begin with, the function of the board has been redefined as an overview role rather than as an active managing function. The purpose of the independent-dominated ideal board is to oversee the business, social, and legal activities of the senior management. Thus management will be monitored by an independent group, instead of being free to "review" its own handiwork, as in the case of a management-dominated board. For example, if management fails to achieve expected profit results, the board will ask intelligent questions, request new efforts, or, if necessary, hire new senior management. Likewise the board will oversee the efforts of management to comply with law and appropriate ethical standards of business behavior. The board will lay down general guidelines and evaluate results. It will not manage, because that is a proper role for management which is in the trenches from day to day. An essential and crucial element of the new board function is the enhanced importance of the independent directors. Indeed, the former chairman of the Securities and Exchange Commission, Harold Williams, has recommended that all members of the board, with the exception of the CEO, should be outside directors.[6] Independent directors are individuals who have no material present or past ties to the corporation. They should not be officers or employees of the corporation. They should not be legal counsel to the business. Their occupations and businesses should have no relationship to the corporation. Since they are independent it is assumed that they will be able to oversee vigorously the actions of senior management and ensure that management maximizes the welfare of shareholders.

The role of independent directors in the reform movement is reinforced by reliance on a strong committee system. The three most important committees are audit, compensation, and nominating. The audit committee is a group of directors charged with the responsibility of monitoring the selection and performance of the independent certified public accountants who audit the books of the corporation.[7] This committee interposes itself between the outside accountants and management so as to assure that the accountants are truly independent and are honestly and effectively forcing management to disclose the financial status of the corporation. Needless to say, the reformers insist that the audit committee be dominated by, or better yet made up exclusively of, independent directors.[8]

The compensation committee is a group of outside-dominated directors who are given the authority and responsibility to determine the shape and contour of salary and fringe benefits to be paid to the senior management.[9] In that way the theory assumes that management will not, as Berle and Means and others feared, reward itself unduly at the expense of shareholders.

The nominating committee is designed to increase shareholder democracy. Because of its control over the proxy machinery, management in effect selects the members of the board. Therefore, the SEC and others have recommended the formation of nominating committees composed of independent directors that would have either the responsibility to recommend to the full board or perhaps the power itself to nominate directors for election by the shareholders at the annual meeting.[10]

Related proposals have also been made to emasculate further management's control over the election process. One suggestion would require the corporation to subsidize the election slates of shareholders in opposition to the incumbent board. This proposal might establish by statute, for example, that every group of 100 shareholders could at corporate expense nominate and solicit shareholder votes and proxies.

We will examine these new proposals in detail in later sections of the book. Suffice it to say at this point that there is no empirical evidence that independent directors benefit shareholders and there is ample indication that part-time outside directors may be so disinterested in the fortunes of the corporation as to minimize rather than maximize profits for shareholders. This book will demonstrate that all of those proposals would politicize the corporation, ruin its efficacy, and thwart the real desires of shareholders.

Recommendations have also been made to strengthen the duty of loyalty and care concepts. Some writers have recommended federalization of the duties of loyalty and care by way of a comprehensive and tough federal statute to replace the 50 different state bodies of law.[11] This book will critically examine these concepts and conclude that there is no established empirical connection between the legal notions of "care" and management behavior, and no meaning to the phrases "fairness" or "loyalty" in the corporate law context. They are, to use a term from F. A. Hayek, a "mirage."[12]

RADICAL REFORMERS

The more radical reformers would not rest with these changes.[13] They would reconstitute the board by requiring that it include representatives of outside interest groups, so-called constituency directors. Representatives of consumers, environmental groups, small businesses (e.g., auto dealers in the case of General Motors), local communities, labor, and minority groups would by some statutory formula be placed on the board. At the same time the board would be required to maximize the welfare of "society" rather than the corporation's shareholders, a notion commonly called corporate social responsibility. Government agencies would define the needs and desires of "society" and perhaps governmentally appointed directors would be appointed to the board to ensure the "socialization" of the corporation. These concepts, which are obviously difficult to specify—for example, what is the "interest of society"—would radically transform the modern corporation from a profit-seeking private enterprise into a completely new entity. This book will present a critical analysis of these concepts, but it should be clear that whether or not one agrees with these proposals, they would transform corporations into arms of the state even if they were not formally nationalized.

In the sections that follow we will attempt a new analysis of the corporation. In Part II we will explore the nature of the firm. At the root of corporation law and the Berle and Means thesis is a notion of the corporation as a kind of artificially created autocracy run by a small clique of managers. It is obviously vital to understand the nature of firms and organizations in order to begin to truly understand the corporation. We will explore recent developments in the theory of the firm and apply them to the corporation. In that manner we will demonstrate that the corporation is a natural and useful structure that takes the form it has *because* it benefits shareholders; it is not a form that has evolved to suit the interests of control. In Part III we will examine the effective constraints that the free market imposes on management to force them to act for the welfare of shareholders and the public. In Part IV we will carefully explore the recommendations of the liberal and radical groups to impose "shareholder democracy" and corporate "social responsibility," and to alter corporate law so as to impose additional legal constraints upon management. In Part

III we will also critically assess the efficacy of the nonmarket constraints imposed by the legal doctrines of duty of care and duty of loyalty. In Part V we will evaluate the principal federal corpus of corporate law, securities regulation, much of which was passed in the 1930s because of the influence of Berle and Means and like-minded thinkers, and determine whether those regulations are working well or at all. In a concluding section we will assess the nature and limits of corporate power and social responsibility and the value and morality of corporate profit maximizing.

PART II

Modern Theory
of the Firm

4

Emergence of the Firm

ECONOMIZING ON CONTRACTING COSTS

Berle and Means and their modern followers view the corporation as a system of exploitation of the many shareholders by the few in control. They look upon the law as an instrument of chasten and coerce control. Although the critics of the corporation favor continual efforts at tinkering with the law to strengthen its coercive effect, many are at heart pessimistic about the ability of moderate legal reform to tame control. That is why they are fundamentally in accord in advocating the direct intrusion of the government into the corporate system so as to permanently emasculate the power of private management. They naively assume that government will be more efficient and more honest than private management.

At the heart of Berle and Means's position is a profound misconception of the nature of the corporation. It fails to explain (1) why business firms voluntarily emerge and (2) why they take the form they do. Modern theorists of the firm have demonstrated that the modern corporation is a natural product of the cooperation of shareholders and managers rather than the end result of an exploitative process.

The first of these questions began to respond to analysis with

Coase's 1937 article, "The Nature of the Firm," belatedly recognized as a classic in this field.[1] Coase asked the puzzling question why firms, within which the market system does not operate, arise in a free enterprise market economy. He quoted Salter's description of the market price system: "Over the whole range of human activity and human need, supply is adjusted to demand, and production to consumption, by a process that is automatic, elastic, and responsive."[2] The economic system is coordinated by the price system. Company A sells goods to B at a market price. The transaction takes place openly if both A and B think the price is right for themselves. After the transaction both are better off since each has gotten what he desires. A has received a price he considers "fair." B has acquired goods at a price he considers "fair." If more and more people like B want the particular class of goods, the price will rise. As a result, producers of the factors of production for that class of product will step up the production of the highly demanded goods. In that way the price mechanism allocates resources into products and services that are in high demand. All of this is simple elementary economics. In the real world, however, firms exist within which the market system does not function. As Coase observes, a worker moves from one floor to another because of instructions by a manager, not because of the price system. In a department store the allocation of different sections, such as men's clothes or shoes, could be affected by competitive bidding by independent entrepreneurs for the space. Instead, a department store firm owns the spaces and allocates them by management decision and the use of employees rather than independent contractors. As Alchian and Demsetz pointed out in a more recent article,[3] when a lumber mill employs a cabinetmaker, that is a firm. If the cabinetmaker purchased wood from the mill instead, that would be a market transaction. Why these differences? Why do firms arise? Why does not the market system determine most or all arrangements? Conversely why do markets exist? Why does not one firm eventually absorb the entire economy? Why are resources allocated in some cases by the market and in other cases by the managers of a firm? Of course, the firm intersects with the market. It can survive only if it is efficient and meets the competition of other firms. But decisions within the firm, although ultimately defined by the imperatives of interfirm competition, are made directly by managers, not by a market pricing mechanism.

In socialist states the state nationalizes industry. The state firm arises by political action and by governmental fiat. The same is true for government agencies such as the public school system in American society. In a free-market economy, however, business firms arise voluntarily without state compulsion. In a brilliant piece of insight, Coase concluded that "the main reason why it is profitable to establish a firm would seem to be that there is a cost of using the price mechanism."[4] The cost includes the effort to discover the various market prices and the costs of negotiating the many contracts with suppliers of services and commodities. In a firm, the manager (called the entrepreneur by Coase) negotiates one long-term, indefinite open-ended contract with his suppliers of services or products. The lumber mill in the example given above enters into a long-term contract with the cabinetmaker in which the latter agrees to work and produce at times and within limits to be determined from time to time at the discretion of the plant manager. His duties are understood but they are open-ended in that the plant manager reserves the right to make this decision or that demand from time to time as the circumstances warrant. The limits of the employees' duties are stated, but not the details. Coase concluded, "When the direction of resources (within the limits of the contract) becomes dependent on the buyer in this way, that relationship which I term a 'firm' may be obtained."[5] The long-term contract is the form used, since it is less costly than the alternative market transaction approach. A firm arises when entrepreneurial direction is less costly than market transactions. A firm grows when the cost of managing an additional transaction within the firm is less than that of engaging in a market transaction to accomplish the same result.

Coase's analysis compelled economists to begin looking for particular constraints on free market contracts that might lead to intrafirm rather than market relationships. Klein, Crawford, and Alchian have pointed out that certain assets are "specific" to a firm and hence better owned than leased or rented.[6] They cite the following example:

> An illustrative example is the ownership by automobile-producing companies of the giant presses used for stamping body parts. The design and engineering specifications of a new automobile, for example Mustang for Ford, create value in Ford auto production. The manufacture of dies for stamping parts in accordance with the above specifications gives a value to these dies specialized to Ford, which

implies an appropriable quasi rent in those dies. Therefore, the die owner would not want to be separate from Ford. Since an independent die owner may likely have no comparable demanders other than Ford for its product and to elicit supply requires payment to cover only the small operating costs once the large sunk fixed cost of the specific investment in the dies is made, the incentive for Ford to opportunistically renegotiate a lower price at which it will accept body parts from the independent die owner may be large. Similarly, if there is a large cost to Ford from the production delay of obtaining an alternative supplier of the specific body parts, the independent die owner may be able to capture quasi rents by demanding a revised higher price for the parts. Since the opportunity to lose the specialized quasi rent of assets is a debilitating prospect, neither party would invest in such equipment. Joint ownership of designs and dies removes this incentive to attempt appropriation.[7]

The foregoing analysis, as the authors pointed out, also explains the following important point:

> The owners of a firm (the residual claimants) are generally also the major capitalists of the firm. As we have seen, owners may rent the more generalized capital, but will own the firm's specific capital. This observation has implications for recent discussions of "industrial democracy," which fail to recognize that although employees may own and manage a firm (say, through their union), they will also have to be capitalists and own the specific capital. It will generally be too costly, for example, for the worker-owners to rent a plant because such a specific investment could be rather easily appropriated from its owners after it is constructed. Therefore it is unlikely to be built. A highly detailed contractual arrangement together with very large brand-name premium payments by the laborers would be necessary to assure nonopportunistic behavior. This is generally too expensive an alternative and explains why capitalists are usually the owners of a firm.[8]

MONITORING FUNCTIONS IN THE FIRM

Coase had focused on the factor of transactions or negotiating costs as a determinant of the creation or expansion of firms. Alchian and Demsetz later analyzed the related issue of the shirking-information problem of team production in a firm, a dilemma otherwise known as management discretion or self-interest.[9]

In business firms managers give directions to employees. Those directions cannot be effective unless the manager has information about the diligence of the employee. The worker may in her own self-interest prefer the easy life. If she can get away with it she may shirk and rely on others in the organization to produce the product that earns the shirker her living. The manager will have to monitor the employee's work to lessen shirking.

The members of a firm engage in a team or joint effort in the production of goods or services. How can the individual members of the team best be induced to work efficiently? Some form of monitoring must be employed to reduce shirking. Individual members of the firm could monitor themselves and the other team members. This is possible in small firms such as partnerships and closely held corporations. Even there each member may slack off and rely on the efforts of other members of the firm. In large organizations with many members, self-monitoring will normally be extremely difficult. The best method is for *one small group to specialize in monitoring the efforts of the other firm members.* For that group to be effective it must have power over the firm and the labor and capital inputs into it. It must be the central group that hires, disciplines, and fires employees. It must have the power to attract capital on the most advantageous terms. It must have the power to select locations of plants and business tactics and strategies.

But how shall the monitor be monitored? The most effective method is to create automatic built-in voluntary incentives to monitor well. A most effective method is to give residual rewards, that is, the ownership of net earnings, less payouts to the other inputs.[10] This will give the monitor a great incentive to check the shirking of firm participants. If there are multiple owners, many of whom do not engage in the monitoring business, the monitoring manager cannot receive the entire residual. The greater his rewards are tied to profits, however, the greater will be his incentive to monitor well. Another method is to develop methods by which outside rival monitors will be rewarded if they replace ineffective incumbent monitors. Another method is to increase the competition within firms for the top monitoring jobs.

Shirking exists in all team efforts.[11] Whenever an employer hires another person to perform services for it, an agency relationship is created. In every case a monitoring arrangement must arise or be established to limit shirking. An agent with an average component of self-interest will not always act in the best interest of the employer. Naturally, employers know this and endeavor to monitor the agent's performance in a way that minimizes the costs of shirking (''agency costs'') to the employer.[12] In fact, the same phenomenon occurs whenever two or more people work together. A coauthor of a magazine article may face the same problem. Author A may sit back, write only one-third of the article, and hope to receive full public recognition and half of the royalties. Author B will have to monitor A's work to prevent these unhappy results.

In large government bureaucracies and universities, employees at all levels may endeavor to maximize their personal comfort at the expense of group efficiency. For example, a government bureaucrat may prefer large offices, congenial associates, and a large staff. Although her supervisors may monitor her work, the high-ranking supervisors may themselves shirk. If citizens had the time and money to detect these actions, they would compel them to produce the same amount of work or more at less cost, or hire others willing and able to do it. But who then should monitor the government bureaucrat? Citizens do not have the time or ability. Since government agencies and universities are not profit-oriented, there is no bottom line profit test to measure management efficiency. Therefore, monitoring of agency costs is more difficult in these nonprofit organizations than in businesses run for profit.[13]

Agency costs also may arise in small or large closely held business corporations, where stockholders share ownership and control. Each shareholder must worry about the shirking of the other owner-managers. But since share ownership is less dispersed than in a publicly held corporation, the active shareholder-manager can more readily check the activities of fellow managers than can a passive small shareholder in a publicly held corporation. There is, therefore, no necessity for a smaller group to specialize in monitoring. In addition, monitoring is worth more to the close corporation shareholder than to the public shareholder in that the close corporation shareholder-manager usually has more to lose if his monitoring fails. Since individual shareholders own only a fraction of the firm, however, their monitoring may be inefficient. One shareholder may depend on the efforts of other shareholders to work or to monitor. The larger the number of shareholders, the more inefficient will be shared monitoring. Legal doctrines of agency responsibility and duty of loyalty exist between shareholders in the closely held corporation as a result of, or in reaction to, the existence of agency costs. The legal doctrine, however, is not the key factor in close corporation planning. The principal task of close corporation lawyers is to arrange the charter, bylaws, and shareholder contracts so as to share control effectively among the shareholders and prevent shirking. The latter arrangements are not available to public corporations. Indeed, a lawyer who leaves his shareholder-clients in a closely held corporation to the remedies of fiduciary duty, without attempting to structure the corporation to protect them, is open to severe criticism because of the uncertainties and cost of duty-of-loyalty litigation. The same observations in this paragraph holds true for the general partnership form.

APPLICATION OF THE THEORY OF THE FIRM TO THE PUBLICLY HELD CORPORATION

The closely held corporation, the general partnership, and the government-owned firm all share one grievous disability. They do not enjoy the benefits of a public market for their ownership shares. General partners and shareholders in a closely held corporation cannot readily sell their interest. They are locked in. Nor is there a public market for those within the firm who hold the monitoring function. The publicly held corporation is uniquely different. It enjoys a public market for its ownership interest as well as a competitive market for the monitoring function, that is, the tender offer.

The large publicly held corporate firm takes its particular organizational structure not accidentally but because it is the best method of attracting large amounts of capital with a minimum of agency costs. The shareholders are willing investors of capital. The directors and senior management monitor the work of employees and coordinate all inputs of capital and labor into the firm. The investors have voluntarily entrusted management authority to the senior officers who are *specialists* in *monitoring*. The shareholders want the management to maximize the welfare of shareholders to the same extent as would the shareholders if they managed the corporation. But will the monitors shirk? Some of-

ficers may wish to lead the quiet life. They may opt for carpeted
hallways, beautiful secretaries (or handsome ones) and five-hour
workdays. They may be reluctant to take appropriate entrepreneurial risks. Shareholders cope with that problem in a number of ways. Limited liability limits their risks. The stock market
permits shareholders to sell out whenever they wish and invest in
better-run corporations (obviously something not possible in the
governmental firm). The free markets for control through hostile
tender offers permit outside rival managements to displace incompetent, incumbent managements. (This is absent in govern-
ment-run concerns; no one can oust the management of the U.S.
Post Office through a tender offer.) Shareholders benefit from
compensation packages which tie management to profit production (again something not possible in the governmental firm).
Incumbent managements face intrafirm competition from ap-
plicants for their jobs (i.e., the market for management) (again
something which does not work in government with its civil-
service, life-tenure structure). Management is better able to attract capital to the firm by notoriously signaling their honesty
through such important safety devices as retaining independent
certified public accountants to audit their books.

    Throughout the past half century large corporations owned by
thousands or tens of thousands of dispersed shareholders have increased in relative importance. This has occurred although no
government agency has forced shareholders to invest. Large,
family-owned or family-dominated corporations have radically
declined in number and significance. No other form of firm, including the employee-owned corporation, has been remotely as
successful. The publicly held corporation has met and passed the
test of survivorship. There are several reasons for this success. To
begin with, manager-proprietors are frequently unable to finance
large-scale business expansion entirely out of their own funds.
They must often raise some debt and equity capital from individual and institutional sources to improve and expand their
business enterprises. The corporate firm with its freely trans-
ferable shares is superbly organized for this purpose. The other
side of the coin is that public investors find it prudent and rewarding to place their capital under the control of expert and experienced corporate monitors. As Berle and Means noted, their
investment is liquid because of the public market for their stock.
Although there are agency costs involved, it is obviously worth-

while to small public shareholders to hire managers to run business enterprises rather than actively participate themselves.

The existence of agency costs does not mean that the dispersed-shareholder corporate enterprise is inefficient. *The costs are an unavoidable price of joint activity or organization. The alternative for shareholders is actively to manage the business. That alternative would be an obvious absurdity.* Even then, as in the case of coauthors of a book, some agency costs would be incurred. The only viable alternative is for one person both to own and to run the firm.

In short, the modern corporation—with its widely dispersed shareholders—is an inevitable result of the willingness and desire of tens of thousands of relatively small investors to entrust their money to skilled, hired managers. It is also a natural product of the desire of large institutional investors, who have no urge or ability to manage the business, to put their finances in the hands of expert corporate officers. Further, the centralized control by senior management is a natural product of the need to reduce shirking and minimize agency costs. The separation of ownership from control is the inevitable product of the need to maximize managerial efficiency in the corporate firm. The separation is a positive benefit rather than a problem. The existence of public markets which permit rival monitoring groups to take over corporations and displace inefficient shirking incumbent monitors, forces the monitor to monitor well.

Professors Jensen and Meckling, in their seminal piece on the firm, pointed out that critics who complain that agency costs are positive (i.e., nonzero) and therefore wasteful are engaged in what Professor Harold Demsetz called a "Nirvana" species of analysis.[14] Of course, if agency costs could be reduced or eliminated by shareholder monitoring of management at a cost that were less than the benefits derived, the course of action would be simple and clear: always increase the curbs on management. Monitoring, however, is costly and at various levels may not be worth the benefits obtained. Governmentally mandated monitoring in the form of judicial or statutory law and doctrines must always be measured against the cost-benefit test. Too often, as shall be demonstrated in this book, the cost impact of corporate law is totally ignored.

Furthermore, given the efficient nature of the capital markets, it is likely that the price of shares has been discounted for agency costs. There is considerable economic literature demonstrating that the efficient stock market impounds in the price of shares all significant public information about corporations.[15] Data on quality of management, financial stability, and quality of products are rapidly diffused to investors with almost immediate impact on the price of the stock.[16] There is good reason to believe that the same phenomenon occurs as a result of investors' awareness of the possibility of manager shirking. Indeed, the work of Jensen and Meckling makes a formal demonstration of such a phenomenon.[17] Their conclusion is that shareholders invest in such corporations because the benefits from the corporate operation outweigh the disadvantage of agency costs.

OWNERS OR RISK TAKERS

There is an even more fundamental objection to the "separation of ownership and control is evil" hypothesis. This issue is the product of an erroneous perception of the concept of the corporation. This perception views shareholders as "owners" who in some way have given up control over their business to a group of self-seeking shirkers. *Shareholders are not owners; they are risk takers.*[18] According to the teachings of modern portfolio theory the most efficient way to invest savings is to diversify holdings. As a result, shareholders invest relatively small holdings in many corporations. Other individuals and groups also make their inputs into each corporation. Labor provides services. Others sell raw materials to the business. Management coordinates the activities and inputs of these groups.

The business firm is a complex of contractual arrangements among the owners of the various production inputs. Managers agree to work for a specified return which normally varies with the success of the enterprise. The managing monitor attempts to raise capital on the most advantageous terms. She pays interest, that is, a fixed return to bondholders. She pays a different kind of return to shareholders: high returns if the firm succeeds, small—possibly negative—returns if the firm fails. The shareholders are similar to bondholders except that they are more optimistic. The residual claim on earnings of shareholders is not a reward for their monitoring; it is simply a kind of return similar in purpose to that of bondholders. Shareholders are thus really similar to bondholders. They have as little interest in voting rights as do bondholders. Their only interest is that the monitors manage the enterprise well. Small shareholders have little or no interest in the vote. They are interested in dividends and capital gain. Their vote, as we will see, is important only in that it facilitates the market for control via tender offers and occasional proxy battles for control.

CONCLUSION

The traditional corpus of corporate law described in Chapter 1 and the reforms outlined in Chapter 3 all flow from a fear of the separation of ownership from control. That notion is based upon a mistaken belief that control is somehow an artificial element that has grown into prominence at the expense of shareholders. Actually the corporate firm has evolved as a result of shareholder desire to enjoy the advantages of the separation phenomenon. The shareholders have entrusted power to control in order to maximize their return. Corporate control or management personnel are specialists in monitoring. If they did not exist or if they disappeared they would have to be created in order to satisfy the investment desires of shareholders. Unlike management in government they are forced to monitor efficiently because of the efficient public stock market, described in the next section of the book, that swiftly disciplines inefficient monitors.

Since management is forced to manage efficiently, the publicly held corporation pursues the same goal that the historic Adam Smith classical entrepreneur pursued: the maximization of profit by satisfying consumer demand. The system of senior management in the large publicly held corporation, therefore, is a positive benefit rather than the disadvantage that Berle and Means perceived. The remarkable fact is that in their efforts to place judicial and governmental restraint on the structure, corporate law reformers are frustrating a process that has evolved as a result of natural forces that operate for the benefit of shareholders and the public.

PART III

Free Market and Nonmarket Constraints on Manager's Discretion

5

Markets for Control, Management, and Products

MARKETS FOR CONTROL

The separation of ownership and control is not some corporate original sin; rather, such a model is the natural and spontaneous choice of tens of thousands of shareholders who are looking for successful investment vehicles. Public shareholders do not have the time, knowledge, experience, or desire to manage corporations, whereas officers and directors are skilled in managing businesses. The separation of ownership and control is thus a natural and efficient phenomenon.[1] The success of the widely held corporation is evidence of the efficiency of the model: the great majority of large corporations are characterized by widespread, dispersed public share-ownership, with a separate control group of managers. Only in a relatively small minority of cases are very large publicly held corporations characterized by a dominant family control group.

Naturally, the fact that the public shareholder corporation is an efficient investment medium is not proof that corporate directors never shirk their duties to shareholders or engage in gross forms of dishonesty. The free markets for control and management, however, operate to limit management abdication of responsibility. Modern portfolio theory teaches individual and institutional investors to diversify their holdings in numerous corporations and to hold the stock only as long as the market price of the stock rises, or at least as long as it does not fall. Furthermore, modern learning on the efficient market has concluded that the price of the stock reflects all of the material, publicly available information about the corporation.[2] The efficient market is an astoundingly rapid collector of and responder to bits and pieces of information about a company. Indeed, economists have demonstrated that pertinent information has usually been received and evaluated by the market long before it is dispersed through SEC-mandated documents and reports.[3] Therefore, inefficient or dishonest corporate managements will have a rapid impact on the price of that corporation's stock; its price will fall. It will fall because of the elementary but fundamental fact that shareholders sell out when they learn that corporate management is incompetent or dishonest.

The importance of market reactions to corporate management can be emphasized by comparing a shareholder to a citizen of Connecticut, for instance. If the latter does not like the action of his governor or his legislators, either he can attempt to vote them out of office by utilizing the electoral process, or he can leave the state. Changing governors or a state assembly is a difficult process at best, however, and since leaving the state would involve changing jobs and moving spouse and children, no real alternatives are available. The shareholder's situation is drastically different. Shares can be sold easily at the first sign of significant management incompetency or dishonesty. This phenomenon, known as the "Wall Street Rule," nullifies many of the objections to the separation of ownership and control. Alternatively, shareholders may consider waging a battle to change management, although this is an expensive and difficult strategy, hardly worth the effort to most shareholders who have relatively small holdings in any one corporation.

The ease with which shareholders can transfer investments does not mean that incumbent management is free to continue feathering its nest at the expense of the remaining shareholders. As Manne has demonstrated, a dishonest or incompetent management team will cause the corporation to become vulnerable to outsiders seeking to acquire corporate control.[4] When the price of a badly run corporation drops, it becomes an attractive target for a takeover by other groups who believe that they will be able to manage the corporation more efficiently than the incumbent management. Although raiders will pay a premium over the current market price of the target company stock, the premium is paid in the belief that as a result of their superior management the price will recoup to a level in excess of the premium. There is, therefore, a powerful incentive for incumbent management to strive to maximize shareholder profits. Only if government regulation makes takeovers more difficult can management indulge in greater shirking and dishonesty.

It may be argued that target companies are frequently efficiently run and that the takeover group retains management after takeover of the target company. As Easterbrook and Fischel have pointed out, this amounts to "second guessing the market. Unless the acquirer is giving away its money, the premium price paid for the shares indicates a real gain in the productivity of the assets."[5] The subjective belief that the "acquired firms are well run does not exclude the possibility that, in new hands, the firms would be better run."[6]

The fact that management is retained is not significant. As Easterbrook and Fischel argue, "they often lose effective control to officers of the acquirer."[7] In any event, empirical data quoted below indicate that prices of target corporations decline relative to the market prior to the offer, hence indicating less than optimal behavior.

It has also been argued that tender offers hurt long-term planning and, therefore, harm the economy. Again, Easterbrook and Fischel answer this argument conclusively when they point out that "if the market perceives that management has developed a successful long term strategy, this will be reflected in higher share prices that discourage takeovers."[8] Although the risk of takeovers creates management insecurity, that tends to spur efficient behavior, not the reverse.

Others have argued that tender offers divert capital from investment into useless rearranging of the ownership of already existing corporate property and assets. This ignores the fact that the acquisition will result in a better use of resources than payout of offeror's cash dividends, or offeror internal investment. As Easterbrook and Fischel have forcefully pointed out, this position "would deny shareholders the right to the most profitable rate of return by forcing firms to make new capital outlays when a takeover or merger would be more profitable."[9]

It has also been argued that tender offers merely create self-aggrandizing corporate empires. This argument assumes that product competition and the market for control do not discipline corporate mangement. Easterbrook and Fischel have noted that a self-aggrandizing management team that did not maximize shareholder return ''would have lower share prices. . . . The corporation itself would become a takeover candidate.''[10] Although some would argue that takeovers create monopolies, Easterbrook and Fischel have concluded that ''most tender offers raise no antitrust problems, and one careful study has shown that takeovers generally reduce concentration in the acquired firms' markets.''[11]

Finally, Easterbrook and Fischel have summarized conclusive empirical studies which indicate that takeovers discipline management and increase welfare. Their conclusion is worth quoting at length.

> The raider, managerialist, and monopolist models of tender offers are also contradicted by data on stock price movements. Most of the movement in the price of a stock is correlated with movement in the market as a whole and depends on general economic conditions. But the movements in individual stock prices net of movements in the market give a rough picture of the fortunes of the issuing companies, and data about these movements for individual companies—called cumulative average residuals, or CAR's—are powerful indicators of a company's performance.
>
> Each of the views of tender offers, including the welfare-maximizing view that we advance, implies a particular pattern of acquirers' and targets' CAR's. The proposition that tender offers move assets to better uses implies that, because the acquirers are looking for targets with suboptimal performance, the prices of the targets' shares would decline relative to the market for a period prior to the offer. The targets' CAR's would begin to rise again, shortly before the offer was announced, as information leaked to the market. The CAR's of the untendered shares would show significant gains over the preannouncement position. The offeror's CAR's should show little abnormal movement, because offerors should not be able to make more than a competitive return (given the extent of risk) on their investment in the target.
>
> If, on the other hand, tender offers are conducted to raid the assets of the targets, the CAR's of targets would be steady until word of the offer leaked to the market; then they would decrease, as investors feared the worst. The CAR's of the minority, untendered shares would plummet after the acquisitions were completed. The

CAR's of offerors should rise, in anticipation of gains from looting, once word reached the market.

If tender offers harm the acquirers because their management acquires the wrong firms or pays prices that are too high, then the acquirers' CAR's should be steady or declining until word leaks, after which they would decrease. The CAR's of the targets would be steady until shortly before the offer, when they would increase. Untendered shares would not appreciate in price.

Finally, if tender offers are an instrument of monopolization, the CAR's of both firms should be steady before word of the acquisition spreads, and then both CAR's should rise in anticipation of monopoly profits.

A great deal of evidence has been accumulated on the movement of CAR's before and after tender offers. The evidence shows that the CAR's of acquired firms decline steadily for approximately forty months before the offer. A month or two before the offer, they begin to rise. After the offer has been completed, the nontendered shares continue to trade at a significant increase over the pre-offer price. The CAR's of the offerors rise when the offer is made. The estimates of gains to targets' shareholders run from 14% to 50%; the estimated gains to offerors' shareholders are 5% to 10%.

In the judgment of the market, then, tender offers increase welfare. They rescue firms with declining CAR's but do not hurt the acquiring firms. Most of the gain goes to shareholders of the target, who benefit whether or not they tender. After the acquisition has been completed, the minority untendered shares of the target continue to trade at prices significantly higher than the pre-offer price. The acquiring firms' prices increase continuously before the acquisition—not the pattern we would expect if bidders were managed by self-aggrandizing men. This pattern of security prices is inconsistent with the raiding, managerialist, and monopolist views of tender offers but is consistent with the value-maximizing approach that we adopt.[12]

More recent data generally confirm Easterbrook and Fischel's conclusions, although these data establish that gains to the offeror's shareholders may be lower than stated above. Jensen summarized the evidence as follows:

The evidence on the stock price effects of takeovers . . . has been painstakingly collected by the authors of over a dozen studies in the past five years. It shows the abnormal stock price changes for firms involved in takeovers. Abnormal price changes are stock price changes that have been adjusted to eliminate the effects of market-wide price movements. As the [data show], target firm shareholders earn the lion's share of the gains in takeovers—30% in tender offers and 20% in mergers. Moreover, since these abnormal stock price changes do not take full account of the purchase premiums, average target stockholder returns in takeovers are actually higher than these estimates. Bidding firm shareholders on average earn about 4% in tender offers and nothing in mergers. If there is raiding or piracy taking place it seems to be a peculiar "Robin Hood" variety. . . .[13]

For a number of technical reasons Jensen further concluded that future studies will show

> that the returns to bidders in mergers are actually more like the 4% shown for tender offer bidders than the zero estimate. . . .[14]

The empirical studies, therefore, demonstrate that tender offers greatly maximize value for target shareholders. The data indicate that tender offers are value-maximizing, consistent with the theory that the market for control disciplines incompetent management and inconsistent with a theory that bidders generally engage in "piracy."

MARKETS FOR MANAGEMENT

Another incentive of the control group for maximizing shareholder profits is termed the "market for management." Fama has persuasively argued that a manager's future compensation package depends upon her reputation for efficiency and honesty.[15] This is true with respect to reputation without as well as within the corporation. Such a conclusion should be no surprise to practicing attorneys or business executives who are personally aware of the rapidity and efficacy of adjustments in the market for highly regarded attorneys and managers. Corporate managers similarly have an incentive to monitor the performance of their superiors. The reputation of the senior manager will redound to the benefit or detriment of his subordinates. Empirical studies confirm this intuitive theory and demonstrate that inefficient executives are soon fired.[16]

MANAGEMENT COMPENSATION

The crucial proposition of the Berle and Means thesis is that the interests of management and stockholders diverge widely. Hence, management can be expected to pay itself more compensation than it would receive in owner-dominated corporations. As we have demonstrated in Chapter 2, Berle and Means presented no scientific empirical evidence in support of their proposition. Despite that, the book emphasized the fear of corporate mis-management by officers.

In a recent study, Nobel Laureate George J. Stigler and an associate pointed out that for many years there was no "serious attempt by anyone to discover whether the main tenets of *The Modern Corporation* were correct." [17]

In 1983 Stigler and Friedland tested the Berle and Means data. Three bodies of data had been available in the 1930s to test the Berle and Means thesis on executive compensation. The Federal Trade Commission had compiled one set of data:

> In 1933 a Senate resolution requested the Federal Trade Commission to collect salary schedules of officers and directors of large corporations listed on the New York Stock Exchange. Data on compensation . . . were collected retroactively through 1928 and they are the basis of the present section. . . . A regression of salaries . . . reveals no relationship of compensation to type of control. . . . A comparable analysis of the data for 1931–32 again shows no relationship of compensation to type of control. [18]

Stigler and Freidland also compared the percentage changes in the corporate bottom line and in management compensation from 1928–29 to 1931–32. They pointed out:

> The literature commonly asserted that officers could set their own compensation rather independently of the corporation profitability. The early years of the Great Depression offer no support for this hypothesis. . . . There was a weak positive association between the two variables, but the type of corporate control had no significant effect upon it. [19]

Stigler and Friedland then pointed out that in 1936 a second set of data on executive compensation appeared, this set collected by the Securities and Exchange Commission. They obtained the average compensation of the two best-paid officers in 77 of the 106 industrial corporations in the Berle-Means tabulation. Stigler and Freidland compared the

> combined compensation of the two highest paid executives against the logarithm of total assets of the firm in 1934–35. . . . In the figure, each corporation is again distinguished by whether it is

owner or management controlled according to Berle and Means. The relationship between executive pay and type of control is non-significant and negative. . . .[20]

Next, Stigler and Friedland used Temporary National Economic Committee (TNEC) data for 1937 and SEC data for 1937–38. Their conclusion was that "again we find no relationship between executive pay and type of control. . . ."[21]

RAISING OF CAPITAL

There is yet another feature of corporate activity that automatically curbs the excesses of management. Publicly held corporations often need to raise capital through the sale of stock and therefore have a financial interest in raising the market price of their stock. Moreover, corporations use stock for many other purposes, including management compensation, business acquisitions, and funding pensions. Thus, the benefits of retaining a high price for the securities of a corporation inure to management as well as shareholders. Because of the desirability of maintaining a sound market for the corporation's stock, management has an incentive to signal potential and current investors that the officers and directors of their corporation are honest and efficient.[22] That purpose is accomplished by the voluntary release of ample financial data and the retention of outside accounting monitors of corporate conduct to reassure public investors' faith in the data.[23]

OWNER- AND MANAGER–DOMINATED FIRMS

In recent years there has been an effort in the economic literature to compare empirically the performance of owner- and manager-dominated firms in order to test the theory that managers shirk more (i.e., do not strive to maximize shareholder welfare) than owners of family-dominated firms. The evidence has been very mixed. Indeed, Herman in a recent empirical study found no relationship between any measures of earning rates and the type or structure of control.[24]

The aforementioned Stigler and Friedland study also examined this issue as it bore on the actual Berle and Means list of corporations. Stigler and Friedland stated:

> The type of corporate control was asserted to have an important influence upon the goal of management. The owner-controlled corporation would seek maximum profits, while the management-controlled corporation would [not] . . . because . . . large profits little benefitted the management.[25]

Stigler and Freidland then analyzed the Berle and Means list of corporations and did not find "any effect of type of control."[26]

The best recent empirical evidence, therefore, does not show that the separation phenomenon creates significant management sloth, indolence, or other forms of shirking. One would expect that family-dominated firms would have better performance than management-dominated firms, at least if one believes the Berle-Means thesis. The evidence does not bear this out.

In talking about competitive effects, we cannot, of course, avoid product competition. Even the largest American corporations are working in a fiercely competitive economy that swiftly punishes a failure to satisfy the consumer. The American automobile industry is painfully learning that lesson today.[27] Management perishes when it does not produce competitive products and succeeds when it does. The shareholder benefits when management is successfully entrepreneurial and suffers when it is not.

SEPARATION

Our discussion thus far assumes that ownership of the modern corporation is "so diluted among the multitude of shareholders that their interests are essentially unrepresented when corporate management makes its decisions."[28] We have developed scientific empirical answers to that charge. We have referred to, for example, markets for control, management, and data on executive compensation. In a recent study Demsetz demonstrated that the root assumption of significant separation is suspect. As he put it, "ownership and control are not so separate as is often supposed."[29]

To begin with, he pointed out,

> a substantial fraction of outstanding shares are owned by directors
> and management of corporations in all but the very largest
> firms. . . . An average of twenty firms, ten in the middle and ten at
> the bottom . . . reveals that corporate managers owned about 20
> percent of outstanding shares. . . .[30]

He then pointed out that although in the ten largest firms, as
of 1975, the average management share was about 2 percent,
"the value of managers' holdings in the largest corporations is
roughly twice the average of other smaller manufacturing
firms."[31]

Demsetz noted that a Senate report indicates that the average
largest stockholdings in 122 major corporations is somewhat more
than 20 percent. Demsetz then concluded:

> From these data, it is possible to supplement the management
> shareholdings with outsider shareholdings for the ten largest
> firms . . . so that, when outsider ownership of shares is taken into
> account, all groups of firms . . . including the largest . . . exhibit
> substantial sources of profit-motivated control.[32]

Finally, Demsetz discussed the importance of managers'
equity-based compensation as contrasted to straight salary. He
referred to a study by Wilbur G. Lewellen,[33] who concluded that
equity-type rewards to leading executives in 50 of the country's
largest manufacturing corporations amounted to more than four
times the after-tax income received from nonstock wages.[34]
Lewellen also concluded that for the top five managers, equity-
based compensation was almost five times as large as wages.[35]

CONCLUSION

The dismal separation phenomenon described by Berle and his
followers is collapsing under the weight of recent findings. It is not
even true that the separation phenomenon ever existed, at least to
the extent pictured by Berle and his followers. In any event, on
analysis, the so-called disadvantage of separation of ownership
and control is merely one example of the inevitable cost of any
form of joint effort. Universities, government bureaucracies, and
coauthors of law review articles all "suffer" agency costs. Government bureaucracies, however, do not enjoy the same free mar-

ket constraints on managerial discretions that corporations do. The competitive markets for products, management, and control all tend to limit sharply the ability of, or incentive for, managers to shirk. Indeed, if managers can demonstrate to shareholders and investors that they are not shirking, the price of corporate shares will rise. Therefore, managers have powerful negative and positive incentives to prove that they are not shirking. Vigorous management will deter takeovers and maximize the value of their corporate stock and hence of their incentive packages which are based upon the price of corporate stock.

6

Critique of Nonmarket Constraints on Manager's Discretion: Duty of Care and Business Judgment Rule

THE LEGAL COMMUNITY—attorney litigators, judges, and legislators—has developed over the years nonmarket constraints on managerial discretion. In Chapter 1 I introduced the reader to such legal constraints. These included the state law doctrines of duty of care and duty of loyalty as well as the laws administered by the Securities and Exchange Commission (SEC). It is certainly not my position that each and every legal constraint is always useless and must be abrogated. What has been lacking in the discussion of the American corporation, however, is a healthy skepticism about the value of nonmarket constraints as compared to market constraints. In this chapter we will critically assess the role of one of the more important state legal doctrines, the duty of care. This area is in great flux currently as various legal and bar groups consider changes in the law, and therefore, I will address general principles rather than technical legal details. I shall, I hope, demonstrate its usefulness, the limits of its efficacy, and the dangerous efforts of the SEC and elements of the bar to expand its reach beyond useful limits. In so doing I will begin to establish the

Material in this chapter is taken with changes from Nicholas Wolfson, "SEC Thinking About Corporate Governance and Accountability: Lessons in Bureaucratizing the Entrepreneurial Corporation," in *Corporate Governance: Past and Future*, pp. 19–22. Copyright © 1982 by KCG Productions, Inc. Reprinted by permission.

need for a healthy balance between the efficiency of free market constraints and the uses and costs of purely legal instruments. I will illustrate how the bar too often—in its distrust or ignorance of free markets, and because of its faith in its handmaiden, the law—needlessly and dangerously seeks to expand sometimes useful legal doctrine to the point of damage to the healthy functioning of the corporation.

THE DUTY OF CARE

The Corporate Director's Guidebook prepared by the Committee on Corporate Laws of the Section of Corporate, Banking, and Business Law of the American Bar Association describes the duty of care as follows: "The corporate director . . . assumes a duty to act carefully in fulfilling the important tasks of monitoring and directing the activities of corporate management."[1] The recent SEC Report on Corporate Governance points out that "most current state statutes which cover the duty of care are modeled upon Section 35 of the [1970s vintage] MBCA [Model Business Corporation Act] [, which] describes the 'care,' 'skill,' or 'diligence' which a director must employ."[2] Section 35 of that MCBA states:

> A director shall perform his duties as a director including his duties as a member of any committee of the board upon which he may serve, in good faith, in a manner he reasonably believes to be in the best interests of the corporation, and with such care as an ordinary prudent person in a like position would use under similar circumstances.[3]

The so-called "business judgment" rule under current court interpretation is not closely distinguished from the duty of care. It is basically a "judicial gloss" on that duty.[4]
The Second Circuit recently stated in *Joy* v. *North:*[5]

> While it is often stated that corporate directors and officers will be liable for negligence in carrying out their corporate duties, all seem agreed that such a statement is misleading. . . . Whereas an automobile driver who makes a mistake in judgment . . . will likely be called upon to respond in damages, a corporate officer who makes a mistake in judgment . . . will rarely, if ever, be found liable for damages suffered by the corporation. . . . Whatever the terminology, the fact is that liability is rarely imposed upon corporate directors or officers simply for bad judgment.[6]

The court set forth the policy for this approach as follows:

> Courts recognize that after-the-fact litigation is a most imperfect
> device to evaluate corporate business decisions. The circumstances
> surrounding a corporate decision are not easily reconstructed in a
> courtroom years later, since business imperatives often call for quick
> decisions, inevitably based on less than perfect information. The en-
> trepreneur's function is to encounter risks and to confront uncer-
> tainty. . . .
>
> It is very much in the interest of shareholders that the law not
> create incentives for overly cautious corporate decisions.[7]

The aforementioned SEC Report (in apparent disagreement
with the *Joy* v. *North* test) concludes that "both state legislatures
and state courts have important roles to play in promoting corporate accountability. The legislature can set standards of director conduct at a high, yet reasonable level. . . . Courts . . . can
respond to this direction."[8] The SEC then threatened federal action, asserting that "many commentators believe that progress is
not forthcoming quickly enough. To the extent commentators
and the public perceive that directors are not being held account-
able through the efforts of state legislatures and the state
judiciary, calls for setting standards on a federal level can only increase."[9] The SEC staff, at another point in its report, stated that
although it was not recommending federal legislation on standards at that time, it believed that if such legislation were enacted
it should be "directed toward raising the standards of care required of directors and providing a federal cause of action for
breaches of such standards, including private rights of action."[10]
More recently, the prestigious American Law Institute, in its
project on corporate governance, has also proposed a major expansion of duty of care obligation and a restriction of the protection of the business judgment rule.[11]

The doctrine in the past played an intelligent and useful role.
Business decisions are judgmental, are not made within the rigid
bounds of a precise model, and are essentially based on uncertain
predictions of the future. They involve a process of thought and
insight and shrewd entrepreneurial guesswork in which no one,
certainly not a judge, has a crystal ball. A harsh duty of care standard would force directors and senior management into an artificial procrustean bed. It would force them into mechanical,
legislative decisions, not better judgment.[12]

On the other hand, a case can be made for some outer limit to directorial stupidity. For example, a board of directors that for no good reason orders the building of a major plant when *all* of the relevant and available feasibility and marketing reports *definitely* conclude that the plant will lose money should be answerable in court to disgruntled shareholders.

Courts, at least in the past, were rightfully reluctant to second-guess corporate management in areas and transactions where no management conflict of interest was present. As such, the duty amounted to a wise judicial refusal to make business judgments from the bench. In fact, the doctrine could best be described as a judicial refusal to second-guess business decisions except in fairly rare cases of management foolishness.[13]

Under the influence of the reformers, however, the SEC, some judges, and others such as the American Law Institute, are moving in the direction of toughening the standard and broadening the areas in which the judiciary will ex post facto criticize and reverse prior acts of management and directors.[14] It is a mare's-nest into which the judiciary, under the pressure of litigation and reformers' misguided efforts, is beginning to tread.

The Business Roundtable, a group of leading business executives, in its cogent criticism of recent American Law Institute (ALI) efforts to increase the scope of duty of care violations, has put the matter so well that I will quote in full their statement on the public policy implications of any such change.

> By proposing to expand the scope of duty of care violations and narrow the protection of the business judgment rule, [the ALI] would upset a delicate balance achieved by decades of judicial decisions. Both the business judgment rule and the corporate version of the ''ordinary negligence'' test evolved as a result of the courts' recognition of three inescapable facts: (1) courts are ill equipped to evaluate the merits of business judgments; (2) directors must not be deterred from taking risks or focusing all their attention on matters that seem crucial at the time by a fear that they will be held liable for decisions gone sour or for failing to concentrate on mundane matters better left to employees; and (3) highly qualified individuals must be encouraged to become directors.[15]

The movement to make standards of care harsher for corporate directors and perhaps provide a federal cause of action for breaches has no basis in empirical data or wise policy. To begin with, there is absolutely no evidence that corporations are in the midst of some epidemic of incompetency or misbehavior. On the contrary, they are enmeshed in an ever-increasing web of government regulation and prosecution that has contributed to the decline of corporate efficiency, fired the furnace of inflation by increasing the costs of their operations, and intruded government more and more into the private sector. Second, the push for so-called higher standards assumes that current standards are not high enough. There is no body of persuasive evidence for that assumption. There are no organized empirical studies that have conclusively explained or demonstrated what level of impact current standards are having on directorial competency. In short, there are no empirical benchmarks effectively measuring the impact of current standards.[16] Without that all future changes will have behavioral effects that are purely guesswork. The reform moves are largely, therefore, the result of the propaganda of a small handful of legal academic critics of the corporate scene, and some allies in the private corporate bar, who will use the increasing legal standards of care and the consequential increase in incidence of litigation to increase the power of attorneys over the corporate community (and not so incidentally increase legal fees). The gradual growth of the SEC regulation, the ever-increasing role of complex corporate litigation involving attacks on directors and management, and recent pressure by the SEC to make corporate attorneys into corporate whistle-blowers[17] all serve to divert corporate management and directors into paper-pushing legal concerns instead of running their businesses.

The SEC argument in essence involves choices of various theoretical alternative standards, none of which have been connected to alternative behavioral results. Some commentators recommend a kind of low threshold negligence test that triggers judicial intervention in a large number of cases. In the past more courts would intervene only in very extreme cases of directorial error. None of the tougher standards recommended by commentators or threatened by the SEC have been tested out. That is to say, there is no knowing whether tougher standards will result in better or worse directorial behavior from the standpoint of the shareholders. The most plausible assumption is that harsher standards will harm shareholders because by definition they mean that judges frequently will replace directors and senior management as arbiters of business judgment.[18]

7

Critique of Nonmarket Constraints on Manager's Discretion: Duty of Loyalty

THE MOST FUNDAMENTAL legal responsibility of directors is the duty of loyalty. The courts apply the doctrine to every corporate transaction in which individual directors have some significant interest. When that self-interest is absent, the courts will apply the more liberal business judgment rule described in Chapter 6.

"The Corporate Director's Guidebook"[1] characterizes the duty of loyalty as one in which the director pledges his "allegiance to the enterprise and acknowledges that the best interests of the corporation and its shareholders must prevail over any individual interest of his own."[2] More particularly, the Guidebook prescribes four specific components of that duty. First, whenever a director has a material personal interest in dealings with the corporation she should disclose the existence of the interest before the board takes action and abstain from acting on the matter herself. Second, she should attempt to resolve conflicting corporate interests *fairly*, with concern for the treatment of any minority shareholder who might be adversely affected. Third, whenever a business opportunity comes to her attention as a result of her relationship to the corporation, she should present it to the corporation before pursuing the opportunity on her own account. Finally, she should deal in confidence in corporate matters until there has been public disclosure.[3]

61

The Guidebook further declares that the "fundamental responsibility of the individual corporate director is to represent the interests of the shareholders" and that the director is not "directly responsible to other constituencies, such as employees, customers, or the community," except as specific responsibilities might be provided by law.[4] It is recognized that "economic objectives will play the primary role" in guiding corporate decisions.[5]

A similar duty is imposed upon controlling shareholders of a corporation. Like the directors, they must commit their allegiance to the business and recognize that the best interests of *all* of the shareholders (including, of course, the minority shareholders) must prevail over the particular interests of the controlling shareholders.[6]

Much of corporate law constitutes a development of ramifications of the "loyalty" obligations of directors and control shareholders to the body of all shareholders.[7] The obligation is frequently characterized as a fiduciary responsibility, with directors and controlling shareholders deemed to be fiduciaries in much the same sense as trustees.[8] The crucial element of the doctrine is *fairness:* the contested transaction must be "fair" to the corporation.

When courts apply the loyalty doctrine they do not defer to directorial business judgment. They exercise their own judicial judgment as to the fairness of the transaction to the corporation. Fairness is a vague concept that millenia of sages have yet to clarify. As we shall see, the judges have, if anything, had less success than the sages.

The purpose of the fiduciary principle is to compel directors and controlling shareholders to manage the enterprise fairly on behalf of all the owners rather than in the interest of the managers or only some of the shareholders. It is essentially a regulatory attempt to minimize the agency costs of separation of ownership and control. As such it must satisfy a number of crucial tests:

1. Does it, in fact, lessen the ability of management to depart from its obligation to maximize shareholder welfare?
2. If it does accomplish this result, does it do so at a cost which exceeds the benefits of the regulatory structure?
3. Is it needed? That is, are the market constraints on management more efficient than regulation and the legal process?

MANAGEMENT COMPENSATION

Consider the doctrine in the context of management compensation. While the director's duty of loyalty is intended to place some restraint upon management indulging its self-interest at the expense of shareholders, the doctrine is notoriously difficult to apply in the area of compensation,[9] since corporate law cannot simulate a "just" compensation package. Only the market can do that.

The question concerning compensation for executives is whether it is rationally related to various past and future indicators of business performance, such as net profits. The typical legal case cannot yield empirically valid answers. For example, suppose a steel executive's salary is 10 percent more than the salaries of apparently similar executives in other steel companies, but that his company is earning less than many other steel firms. In the absence of truly egregious facts proving gross corruption and incompetence, it is impossible in the typical shareholder suit against the corporation and executives to decrease his compensation, to determine if, for example, the steel corporation chose the executive best suited to holding unavoidable losses to a minimum? Did the corporation attract the executive best fitted in the long run to solve the problem? Is the excess compensation necessary to attract a manager to a business which for various reasons may be a less attractive place to work than other companies? Is the corporation performing poorly because of factors beyond the control even of able management? Until such questions are answered, the court is without the means to make a rational judgment. As one judge put it:

> Assuming, arguendo, that the compensation should be revised, what yardstick is to be employed? Who or what is to supply the measuring-rod? The conscience of equity? Equity is but another name for a human being temporarily judicially robed. He is not omnipotent or omniscient. Can equity be so arrogant as to hold that it knows more about managing this corporation than its stockholders? . . .
>
> Yes, the court possesses the power to prune these payments, but openness forces the confession that the pruning would be synthetic and artificial rather than analytic or scientific. Whether or not it would be fair and just, is highly dubious. Yet, merely because the problem is perplexing is no reason for eschewing it. It is not timidity, however, which perturbs me. It is finding a rational or just

gauge for revising these figures were I inclined to do so. No blueprints are furnshed. The elements to be weighed are incalculable; the imponderables, manifold. To act out of whimsy or caprice or arbitrariness would be more than inexact—it would be the precise antithesis of justice; it would be a farce.[10]

When corporate law imposes judicial decision on executive wages it is a form of government price fixing. Such an intrusion into the heart of business distorts demand and supply in the same unfortunate manner as do all other government efforts at setting prices.[11]

In addition, the regulatory apparatus has tremendous costs. The legal process requires the services of attorneys and accountants. The legal expenses are immense. There are also the hidden costs that may occur if management, in fear of lawsuits, keeps compensation at a lower rate than is efficient. That is, if a higher rate of compensation in the absence of fear of lawsuit would have attracted a proportionately greater management effort, the shareholders will have lost as a result of the legal doctrine.

There is an additional problem. The duty of loyalty and obligation of fairness doctrine assumes that the threat of legal process will have a deterrent effect. The basic hypothesis is that the doctrine will result in "better" behavior by corporate executives. If it does not, then the benefit of the corporate law apparatus is nil. It is not sufficient to prove that corporate law holds down wages. It is necessary to demonstrate that the law chills executive compensation to an efficient level. Needless to say, this author knows of no conclusive evidence that the legal doctrine causes "better," that is, more efficient, behavior.

In Chapter 5 I discussed the market for management. I pointed out that corporations are always on the lookout for new executives. Incumbent managers recognize that if they shirk, they will be replaced by better talent.

There is convincing evidence in the economic literature that a firm's profit performance is the key factor in explaining variations in the salaries of corporate executives.[12] The empirical evidence supports the thesis that there is an active market for corporate executives.[13] Able candidates compete for the available positions. "Excess" wages are eliminated by the active competition for positions. Poor performers are replaced by more able candidates who are willing to work at equal or lower salaries.

In a recent paper,[14] Crain, Deaton, and Tollison undertook to determine if the market for corporate presidents is related to profit performance.[15] The researchers related length of service to corporate profits.[16] Their empirical results showed that tenure in office of corporate presidents is positively related very responsively to changes in profits. They concluded that corporations do not generally tolerate poor performance of executives.[17]

In conclusion, both empirical evidence and responsible economic theory indicate that shirking in the form of ''excessive'' compensation is controlled by market forces.

GOING PRIVATE

The ''going-private'' phenomenon is a famous example involving a controversial application of corporate law.[18] The so-called ''pure'' going-private transaction involves a single firm in which the control group desires to eliminate minority shareholders. The goal may be accomplished by a tender offer to the minority shareholders or by a merger or reverse stock split.

The tactic of going private has been opposed by commentators and many courts on the ground that directors or control shareholders violate their duty of loyalty and obligation of fairness to minority shareholders.[19] The argument against going private makes two basic points: first, that the transaction lacks any economic efficiency justification and second, that the control group can dictate the price to the minority shareholders.

First, in the so-called ''pure'' going-private transaction, a single corporation expends corporate funds to buy out the minority group. The transaction never involves the potential synergistic benefits that result from the combination of two independent businesses. Opponents therefore argue that the buy-out is without any economic justification.

In light of the agency cost analysis of corporate structure, this argument fails. In a going-private transaction, the acquiring corporation lessens or eliminates the split between ownership and control. As a consequence, agency costs decrease, and monitoring and its costs in all forms are decreased or eliminated. This is a powerful economic justification for going private. As Jensen and Meckling have stated, ''In general if the agency costs engendered by the existence of outside owners are positive it will pay the . . . shareholders . . . to sell out to an owner-manager who can avoid these costs.''[20] In other words, the newly "gone-private" corporation will be more valuable than the publicly held corporation because of the elimination of the costs of the split between ownership and control. When owner-managers estimate that the resources of the gone-private firm will be sufficient to continue the business successfully, they will frequently cause the corporation to buy out the minority at a price in excess of the prevailing market price of the shares of the publicly held firm. When corporate law prevents that transaction or increases its cost by the imposition of complex legal procedures, the minority shareholders, as well as the public, are hurt. Ironically, many commentators who call for regulatory constraints of the supposed evils of the split between ownership and control bitterly criticize going private.

Second, the arms-length bargaining contention asserts that the control group, in the absence of a judicial fairness doctrine, can unduly influence the price of the cash-out. Opponents assert that this will occur both in the "pure" going-private transaction and in "cash-outs" (i.e., involuntary buy-outs) of minority shareholders in mergers of two separate corporations. Therefore, minority shareholders need a judicial fairness doctrine.

As emphasized throughout this chapter, however, the cost of the judicial process must be weighed against its benefits. Furthermore, the corporate law approach must be measured against the benefits of an alternative free market approach. A corporation that gains the reputation of freezing out minority shareholders at an inadequate price will suffer difficulty in raising equity capital in the future. Potential investors will not buy equity shares, or the corporation will be forced to sell the shares at a lower price. That price will reflect investors' estimates of their potential loss if the corporation goes private. The probability of that adverse impact will act as a powerful deterrent against overreaching by corporate insiders.

In rebuttal, opponents will argue that a corporation may go public and some years later freeze out the minority at a low price based upon a one-shot short-run psychology that says, "Now that I have received public money at ten dollars and the market has since sharply dropped, I will buy back at three dollars, keep the profit, and not worry about my loss of reputation." This will seldom if ever be a rational form of thinking. The corporation can never be certain that it will not need additional equity financing in the future. If it goes private at too low a price, however, it will never be able to obtain adequate financing in the future. Moreover, corporations will compete for better reputations. Corporation X will contract with potential investors to buy them out, if at all, in the future on more generous terms than corporation Y offers.

On the other hand, because complex and costly legal restraints increase the costs of going private, they are likely to produce adverse consequences. Existing minority shareholders will lose the chance to be bought out at a price in excess of current market values.[21] Corporations will be less likely to sell stock to future minority shareholders because of the difficulty of going private in the future. One final consequence is the most certain: As a result of corporations' needs for legal assistance through the bramble bush of state and SEC rules in this area, the corporate lawyers will get wealthier. They will be the chief beneficiaries of such regulation.

CORPORATE OPPORTUNITY

Yet another example of the doctrine of the duty of loyalty is the corporate opportunity rule. Corporate law essentially states that an economic opportunity which comes to the attention of a person because of his corporate position cannot be personally expropriated by that person when the opportunity falls within the type of activity that is pursued by the corporation.[22] For example, assume a corporation is interested in possible business acquisitions of type A. If the president learns of a type-A deal he cannot pursue it himself. He must first offer to his corporation the opportunity to acquire the type-A business. The doctrine may be formulated broadly or narrowly, depending upon the court and the jurisdiction.

The doctrine is largely a product of case law. Assume that the case law doctrine did not exist and that Congress or a state legislature was considering the advisability of establishing the doctrine by statute. The first question should address the extent to which the market accomplishes the desired results. If management followed the practice of appropriating opportunities, shareholders and investors would view this as a form of shirking. The price of the shares would drop. Furthermore, the market for management would reflect the shirking in the form of a lowered value on the future wages of the managers. Management, therefore, would have a strong incentive to advertise, enforce, and follow a policy of conveying all opportunities to the corporation.

Only if managers could successfully hide the fact that they were seizing corporate opportunities for themselves might they possibly follow a different route. Since opportunities come from and are known to parties outside the corporation, there is little reason to believe that even in the short run managers could frequently keep their action secret. Furthermore, other managers have incentives to monitor their superiors since the good reputation of their supervisors will enhance their own reputation.[23]

Even if that is not always true, the question to ask is whether a law would significantly improve directorial behavior at a cost which is exceeded by the benefits to be derived. If the acts are indeed easily hidden, then the legal process could not smoke them out except by use of a considerable force in the form of expensive attorneys and accountants. The cost of litigation, some of it groundless or erroneous, would significantly increase the cost of doing business. This would result in higher prices and lower business productivity.

The doctrine may have other adverse side effects. Judges may be called upon to evaluate whether the opportunity was suitable or worthwhile for the corporation, involving an impossible effort at second-guessing free-market decisions. Alternatively, if the courts ignore the suitability or worth of the opportunity, they could establish a harsh doctrine which loads bad business deals on corporations. The doctrine may chill business development. Vice-President X of the ABC Corporation may wish to develop new business Y. However, he may fear a court will take it from him and put it into ABC where it is really not suitable to be placed. Hence he ignores the opportunity. Hence a new business venture never gets off the ground.

Drafters of a new law as well as proponents of a new judicial doctrine should have some burden of proving that it will accomplish the desired results. Because there is an obvious possibility that the cost of the legal process necessary to implement the opportunity doctrine will be greater than the benefits derived, failure to measure those costs would appear to be irresponsible. The corporate opportunity doctrine has developed by the accretion of case law. It is fair to say that not one of the questions raised in this section has been adequately answered by the courts. This pattern permeates corporate law: Case-made or statutory regulation is imposed upon the corporate system without sufficient regard to empirical data and relative cost or benefit.

PARENTS AND SUBSIDIARIES

The class of cases involving dealings between parent corporations and subsidiaries provides an additional example of the fairness doctrine. The issue frequently turns on whether the parent corporation's actions are "fair" to the minority shareholders of the subsidiary.[24] For example, the dispute may relate to whether the parent should develop deals which include the Venezuelan subsidiary or be free to organize developments in other geographical areas which exclude the Venezuelan subsidiary.[25] In another transaction, a parent may be accused of drawing out an excessive amount of dividends from the subsidiary. This allegedly drains the subsidiary of cash and chills its ability to grow and expand. Minority shareholders, of course, receive their pro rata share of dividends based on the number of shares they hold in the subsidiary. The application of the fairness doctrine is inevitably amorphous and subjective. The payment of large dividends by the subsidiary obviously drains it of cash necessary for business expansion, which may hurt the minority shareholders at least in the short run. It may benefit them in the longer run as the enterprise in its totality prospers as a result of the parent's wise use of resources. The payout of dividends to the parent, however, benefits the larger enterprise, that is, the operation of the parent and its other subsidiaries. The latter action benefits the mass of shareholders of the parent. "Fairness" to the minority shareholders of the subsidiary means *fewer* dividends to the parent. "Fairness" to the parent and its shareholders means *more* dividends to the parent. It is impossible to establish an objective judicial test of fairness; the search for judicial fairness pursues a will-of-the-wisp goal. If the market constraints (e.g., product competition, market for control, and market for management) are operating, the opportunities for management shirking will be limited. Moreover, the cost of the shares held by the minority will reflect at the time of purchase the impact of decisions that may benefit majority shareholders of the parent more than minority shareholders of the subsidiary. Therefore, shareholders' returns on equity may be just as great as returns on the higher priced shares of the parent.

SALES OF CONTROL

When a control shareholder sells his control interest in a corporation, the sale is usually at a premium over market price. For example, if the price of a share of common stock of the XYZ Corporation is thirty dollars a share on the New York Stock Exchange, the control shareholder (owning, say, 35 percent of the issued and outstanding stock), may sell his block at thirty-seven dollars a share to the buyer. Minority shareholders frequently take the position in litigation that the premium represents a corporate asset, that is, the right to control the corporation, which must be shared with all the minority shareholders. They rely heavily on the often-debated thesis of Berle and Means that "the power going with 'control' is an asset which belongs only to the corporation; . . . payment for that power, if it goes anywhere, must go in the corporate treasury."[26]

Probably the most famous case of sale of control is *Perlman* v. *Feldmann*,[27] in which the Feldmann family sold control of the Newport Corporation at a premium to a group of end steel users. The sale was made when steel was in short supply because of the Korean War. Newport was a newcomer in the steel industry, and its physical plant consisted of old installations in the process of being supplemented by newer facilities. Except in times of scarcity, Newport was unable to compete profitably for customers outside its immediate location. The Feldmann family, as the district judge found, had no reason to believe that Wilport, the purchaser, intended to injure or loot Newport. As a result of the purchase, the take-over group acquired the power to buy an assured supply of steel from the steel corporation. The court held that the minority stockholders of Newport could compel an accounting for their share of the premium.[28]

One interpretation of the case is a variant of the corporate opportunity theory. Newport had adopted the "Feldmann Plan" pursuant to which Newton received interest-free cash advances from steel users who in return were assured a source of supply. Further, there was some possibility that Newport could utilize the period of short supply to obtain the good will of customers with whom it was dealing, which patronage might extend into a period when the scarcity ended. These were opportunities, the court asserted, which the sale of control eliminated and for which the premium was paid. One rebuttal to that argument is that the marriage of Newport with its corporate purchaser was advantageous, because Newport would be assured of a customer in the form of its new parent. Another answer is that the market price of the stock already reflected the opportunities. Hence the buyer, having paid for the premium (absent looting for which there is no evidence), could profit only by managing the business better than the seller did.

Another broader interpretation of *Perlman* is that it held that the sale of control at a premium is always per se a sale of a corporate asset which must be shared with minority stockholders. Although the weight of authority in other courts and other jurisdictions would appear to be contrary to such a theory,[29] the sale of control is always circumscribed by legal uncertainties and caveats, and the constant threat of costly litigation. Although courts may intone the rule that sales of control are not per se illegal, the penumbra of the per se theory impels the courts to a very close scrutiny of such transactions.

The fundamental point is the inability of judges and the judicial process to evaluate the relative business advantages or disadvantages of a sale of control. That evaluation is a business decision which should be left to the business process. It might be argued that the original control group of Newport was selfishly interested in the transaction and therefore the court should apply some form of intrinsic fairness test or invoke some per se rule against the sale of control. The crucial point about the sale of control, however, is that the selfishness of the seller cannot result in a transaction unless the new control group purchases. The new control group will not purchase unless it believes in its ability to manage the corporation more profitably in the future. In an efficient securities market, the price of the corporation stock reflects all of the material public information pertaining to the corporation, including management performance.[30] The hefty premium over that price paid for the stock of the old control group is evidence that the new control group believes that it can improve upon the performance of the old, thereby increasing the price of the stock in the marketplace and recouping the premium.

Sale of control is a method by which more efficient management groups may displace less efficient groups. It is frequently a method by which management shirking will decrease, because the new control group will seek to recoup the premium paid for their stock by shirking less than old management. As a result, society will benefit. Furthermore, improved performance will result in an increase in the price of the stock acquired by the new control group. That increase will be reflected in the increased price of the minority shares as well. Sales of control, therefore, will tend to have the same beneficial effects as successful takeover attempts.[31] When corporate law chills the process, minority shareholders are harmed.

CONCLUSION

Essentially, corporate law doctrine on the duty of loyalty is a tool used by the legal profession to displace the free market process. It is a method by which lawyers and judges can regulate prices and other factors of production under the rubric of "fairness." Businesspeople have difficulty recognizing this function of corporate law because the doctrine is clouded in arcane legal jargon.

In addition, corporate law is defective in this area because it has evolved haphazardly without serious attention to cost-benefit analysis and empirical data. The need for empirical findings seems obvious, but has only recently become apparent to the members of the legal profession.

In all areas of corporate law, the fiduciary duty doctrine is permeated by uncertainty and arbitrariness because of its fundamentally impossible goal: to simulate the arrangements that would ensure if shareholders actively managed the business. It is difficult to believe that judges and the cumbersome legal process can act as proxies for shareholder self-interest in efficient management. Judges are not entrepreneurs, nor are they shareholders. They do not ordinarily share the incentives for profit maximization that such groups share. It is unlikely that their interpretations of the duty of loyalty will be consistent with what shareholder-owners would desire. Indeed, the fiduciary doctrine may perversely *increase* the gap between ownership and control because of the inability of the judicial process to effectively simulate the desire of shareholders for maximized profits.

PART IV

Corporate
Governance

8

The Illusions of Shareholder Democracy

UNDER STATE LAW, shareholders elect directors at the annual meeting of shareholders.[1] At that meeting any shareholder can be recognized by the chairman of the meeting and may nominate candidates for the board.[2] That right is purely a formality. Each share normally has one vote. A shareholder with 10,000 shares has 10,000 times the electoral power of a one-share shareholder.[3] A shareholder with 100 shares in a corporation with, let us say one hundred million issued and outstanding shares, obviously would need the support of thousands of substantial shareholders in order to prevail. He will not get it.

Very few shareholders attend meetings in person. They grant the power to vote their shares by giving their consent, or proxy, as it is called, to individuals to cast their votes at the meeting.[4] Management, in advance of the meeting, solicits such proxies on behalf of management's nominees for the board of directors. The cost of the solicitation process for incumbent management under state law is borne by the corporation.[5] Not so for insurgent slates. A shareholder who wants to put up his own slate of candidates must advance the cost out of his own pocket. If he is victorious he may ask the shareholders to reimburse him for his expenses. If he loses he will be out the money.[6] The expenditures are enormous: The direct cost of mailing to tens of thousands of shareholders is huge, but when the costs of attorneys, accountants, and printing of materials are added in, the costs are astronomically high.

The expenditure issue is at the heart of the shareholder democracy issue. Radical reformers such as Ralph Nader want federal legislation to force corporations to subsidize election campaigns for the mass of small shareholders.[7] The legislation could take many different forms. For example it could specify that groups of 100 shareholders could qualify for the largess of the corporate treasury. Another variation could require that only groups of 300 shareholders holding at least 2 percent of the issued and outstanding stock could qualify. The differences are unimportant. The end result would be to politicize the corporation, divert it from its proper ends, harm the small shareholders, and damage or destroy the productivity of corporate enterprise.

In Part III I demonstrated the efficacy of the competitive market for control. Outside management groups expend their own funds or other outside funds to wage cash and stock take-over battles against incumbent management. As a result of the interaction of the efficient market and the market for control the system works well.

The proposals for shareholder ''democracy'' would not support or supplement the market for control. The powerful rival management groups that pursue tender offers have both the interest and the resources to detect incumbent management shirking and to benefit by displacing it. As described in Part III, they see, let us say, a market price of $10 per share, estimate that their superior management skill will result in a market price of $20, and are willing to pay somewhere between $10 and $20 to dislodge incumbent management. They do not need federal legislation to sponsor or supplement this monitoring role.

The shareholder democracy movement is directed at the small shareholder. The large shareholders do not need federal legislation. They play quite well the take-over process described in Part III. As I have demonstrated, that process benefits the small shareholders as well as the large. Large shareholders also use the proxy machinery to wage proxy battles to turn out inefficient incumbent managements. Small shareholders, however, do not have the ability, resources, desire, or incentives necessary to play the reformers' shareholder democracy game.

The ostensible purpose for increasing shareholder power is to strengthen the small shareholders' ability to monitor directly the wealth-maximizing efforts of the managers. Small shareholders, however, have little interest in, or time for, such monitoring. Modern portfolio theory recommends that shareholders diversify their holdings as much as possible. Intelligent investors become relatively small stakeholders in numerous enterprises. An investor who has purchased $500 worth of common stock in each of many corporations has only a limited ability to concentrate on each of his investments. His time is better spent in deciding when to hold, sell, or buy rather than in participating in corporate political contests. Indeed, it would be against his self-interest to devote considerable time to selecting nominees for each board and to join in numerous campaigns for their elections. He has a much better route to investment success. If the price of the stock in a particular corporation falls, he can effortlessly sell his stock and invest elsewhere. Similarly, if the price rises he can sell and make a profit. When enough shareholders sell, a powerful message is transmitted to the anxious managers who closely watch the price movement of the shares. Price drops may be the signal to outsiders to wage a take-over bid to capture control of the corporation in the belief that they can run the corporation better than incumbent management.[8]

This process is a far more rational alternative for the small investor than attempting to wage a proxy battle to overturn management. Even if the corporate treasury subsidized the soliciting effort, the cost of the efforts would exceed the value to be obtained.

First, small shareholders do not have the resources to measure excessive management shirking. They cannot afford to hire expensive accounting, legal, and financial assistance. Rival management groups in the market for control do have the resources and incentive to uncover shirking and capitalize on it by the take-over route. Small shareholders lack the resources and the incentive to play the same game.

Second, the cost of identifying able replacements for the incumbent board are enormous. Small shareholders do not have a sizable enough investment stake to justify the costly efforts necessary to identify and nominate worthy replacements for the old board. The small shareholder will face multiple electoral slates and it will be an impossible job for him to determine whether management is shirking and which competing group has put forward a better slate.

Third, the present system, which relies on the market for control described in Part III, places the responsibility for taking over control on those large shareholders who will bear the cost of the consequences of their take-over. They have a tremendous incentive to monitor well when and if they succeed in the take-over. Small shareholders have little stakes in the outcome and, therefore, little incentive to monitor well if they succeed in the take-over. These three considerations go to the heart of the problem with so-called shareholder democracy. It proposes to subsidize small-shareholder proxy contests, although because of their lack of economic incentive such groups have little interest (or ability) to monitor or detect shirking compared to the major shareholders.[9] It is as if a remote cousin living in California were given control over the affairs of his distantly related family living in Connecticut. Havoc will be the result.

Fourth, efforts to unseat *competent* management will proliferate. In the take-over transaction rival management groups stake large sums to back their belief that they can do better than incumbent management. The empirical results, as I have indicated in Part III, demonstrate that the process is working well. If government legislation forces the corporation to subsidize proxy campaigns, small shareholder groups will attempt to unseat competent management. Since the corporation would bear the enormous cost of solicitation, and the shareholders who take advantage of this would have very small investments in the corporation, they will be able to make a move for the executive suite at little personal cost. In the tender take-over market for control the stakes are large; rival management groups make the expensive move only when they believe they can improve on incumbent management. They succeed only when the efficient market "approves" of their effort by bidding up the price of the target company and the take-over companies.

Fifth, the corporate subsidy will cause the proliferation of groups seeking their own moral and political aims rather than profit maximizing goals. Since the federal legislation will protect their pocket, they will be free to attempt to turn the corporation to political and moral directions of their choosing. The end result will be to lessen rather than increase shareholder returns.

Sixth, the subsidization of small-shareholder power will dilute the worth of large shareholders' investment. Corporate law rightly gives each share one vote. Large shareholders, therefore, have a voice commensurate with their economic investment. If they did not, they would be foolish not to seek more rational alternative investments. The shareholder democracy proposals would be equivalent to giving small shareholders economic-voting power equivalent to larger investors: This will inevitably lessen the incentive of large shareholders to invest in corporations and, given the operation of the efficient stock markets, the price of shares will drop, harming the small investor.

Seventh, the corporate subsidies will be used by groups that are hostile to the free enterprise system to disrupt the efficiency of business to the detriment of shareholders and the public. Many of the groups that have been active in the shareholder democracy drive have no interest in investors or the institution of the private corporation. Instead they are interested in confiscating the wealth of shareholders for what they deem are socially beneficent purposes. It takes little imagination to foresee that they will be most active in transforming the corporation into a battleground for their programs to the loss of the mass of traditional investors.

Eighth, there is no corporate law that forbids corporations from instituting a shareholder democracy provision tomorrow. No corporation of any size has instituted such a system. If that electoral mode were of value to shareholders, management would long ago have instituted the system and have gained competitive benefit, in that the efficient market would have valued the stock of such corporations higher than other comparable corporations.

Ninth, the proposal for automatic reimbursement will put a tremendous financial burden on corporate treasuries.

The essential point missed by the shareholder democracy advocates is that shareholders under the current system have more democracy than can ever be provided by the political system. The key is in the market for shares and the market for control. The small shareholder, as Berle and Means long ago pointed out, has exchanged *control* for the important quality if *liquidity*. When a shareholder is dissatisfied with a corporation she simply sells her shares and moves, if she wishes, into another investment. It is as if the citizen and voter in the State of Connecticut could painlessly, without any transaction costs, leave the state whenever she was displeased with the government. If enough shareholders sell, the price of the stock drops and sends a signal to rival management groups who utilize the market for control to displace inefficient incumbent management. (Unlike the Connecticut analogy, in the

corporate world, as a result of the market for control, the small
shareholders' actions will also discipline and perhaps unseat incumbent management.) It is absurd for the small shareholder to
hold onto her investment while she perhaps fruitlessly tries to
organize her own proxy campaign. While she does that, the price
of her shares may drop and she may have to forego college funds
for her children or a vacation for her family. The small size of her
investment makes that a counterproductive exercise. The small
shareholder diversifies her investments in many corporations and
wisely sells when an investment goes sour. If government attempts to induce her to wage election campaigns, those shareholders with economic motives will ignore the government and
wisely sell. It is the shareholders who have particular religious,
political, or antibusiness motives who will dominate the corpora-
tion-subsidized election campaigns.

CONSTITUENCY DIRECTORS

The movement for more shareholder democracy is a red herring.
The radical reformers have a not-so-secret agenda to weaken the
powers of traditional corporate management and replace it with
direct or indirect government control. The agenda becomes
clearer when one examines a related reform item that is usually
associated with many of the shareholder democracy movements:
constituency directors. The critics of the corporation are not
stupid, they are aware of the fact that shareholders, for the
reasons set forth in this chapter, are generally content with the
system. Indeed, the radical reformers have little sympathy or concern for shareholders. They are after bigger and different game:
the transformation of the free-market corporate system into a
socialist regime. The constituency movement is the "camel's nose
in the corporate door" for such groups. These radical reformers
assert that directors are an "unrepresentative" lot that consists
mostly of industry leaders who are business oriented. They want
the board to include representatives of the local community,
religious leaders, representatives of various special interest
groups, union labor, customers of business—such as automobile
dealers in the case of the auto industry—and government-
appointed directors. Since shareholders will never voluntarily
elect such groups, federal legislation would be enacted to man-

date, by some formula, proper representation on the board. These new groups might be given control over key board agenda items. A related suggestion would give local communities, upon, let us say, request of 3 percent of the shareholders or three members of the board, a veto over specified decisions of the corporation.[10] The state would ultimately have to establish criteria for the decisions of the constituency directors since they would not be guided by market forces.

The various constituencies are characterized by a lack of responsibility or concern for corporate profits or corporate production, and are driven by a mandate to pursue their special interests. Consequently the basis would be established for corporate decline, economic stagnation, and the usual cry for government intervention to solve such problems. Although government intervention will harm shareholders and workers, it will accomplish the ultimate goal of the radical reformers, which is to socialize industry.

Winter has pointed out that the proposals will serve to exaggerate the separation between shareholders and management by putting into power individuals and groups that do not have business agendas.[11] Constituency directors will further the interests of their particular groups, not those of the corporate enterprise. In a subsequent chapter we will examine the dangerous consequences of the most familiar of these programs, the codetermination or labor board, which is strongly influenced by, or in some cases totally dominated by organized labor. The crucial factor is that such changes are aimed at transforming the corporation from a profit-oriented enterprise into something that is imbued with vague utopian ideals of ''society'' or ''community'' or ''distributive justice.'' Those new institutions would destroy the productive genius of the American enterprise and transform it into some dreary simulacrum of Amtrak or the U.S. Post Office.

9

Composition of the Board: Independent Directors

THE NOTION OF independent directors is the main theme song of many staff members of the Securities and Exchange Commission and the traditional reformers in the ranks of attorneys and academe.[1] It is also a concept that has received the blessing of many in the business community.[2] There are differences: a former SEC chairman would like to see all of the board, except the chief executive officer, made up of independent directors.[3] Although some in the business community would go that far, many support having a significant number of independent directors on the board but not necessarily a majority. The Commission has attempted to implement its approach by disclosure techniques that highlight the existence or nonexistence of independent directors in a context that implies that independence is a virtue and the lack of it a vice.[4] Very many influential legal and business commentators have proposed that the principal board function reflect a so-called monitoring or overseeing model.[5] This is a model or type of

Parts of this chapter are taken with changes from Nicholas Wolfson, "SEC Thinking About Corporate Governance and Accountability: Lessons in Bureaucratizing the Entrepreneurial Corporation," in *Corporate Governance: Past and Future.* Copyright © 1982 by KCG Productions, Inc. Reprinted by permission.

structure in which the board does not actively manage the business. Instead it chooses senior management, consents to and oversees important corporate plans and policies, evaluates trends and bottom line achievements, and holds senior management responsible for producing acceptable results.[6]

The key mechanism to implement this board model is a board with a majority of "outside" or independent directors.[7] In addition, there are audit committees consisting entirely of independent directors and also compensation and perhaps nominating committees, all dominated by outside directors.[8]

The traditional concept is based upon the philosophy that the Berle and Means separation of ownership from control reaches its extreme in a board that is dominated by senior management. The officers on the board, by virtue of their powers qua directors, will be able to measure their own performance and monitor their own actions. Since the traditional reformers view the corporation as a ministate rather than as a competitive business organization disciplined by the markets for control and management, they want the powers of management to be emasculated by independent directors. These directors have been variously defined by all the many groups that have endorsed the concept, but in essence they are individuals who have no material ties to the corporation. One definition might exclude counsel to the corporation, past officers, suppliers, major customers, investment bankers, and all of their close relatives. All of the definitions, of course, exclude current officers and employees of the corporation. The various definitions are unimportant for our purposes. *The fundamental design of the reform is to place control over the corporation in the hands of the people whose major interests are elsewhere.* Stated so accurately and baldly the proposition sounds fairly idiotic but it is, we must assure the reader, the most widely accepted reform effort of the past decade.

As with most traditional liberal reforms of the corporation, the empirical underpinnings of the proposals are nonexistent. There are no empirical findings that independent directors manage corporations more honestly or efficiently than management boards. In fact the only empirical studies done to date indicate that there is no empirical economic evidence to support the notion that independent directors will increase economic efficiency or promote law compliance.

The Business Roundtable asked Paul W. MacAvoy, then distinguished Professor of Economics at Yale University, to test the American Law Institute proposals for independent directors and key committees dominated by independent directors. He used a group of some 495 large corporations and tested corporate economic, legal, and social performance. He found that the independent director model had no success in accomplishing economic and legal goals. First, with respect to economic success, Professor MacAvoy empirically showed that "the most important and statistically significant result is that there is no indication here that the board structure has any impact on the relative profitability performance of corporations."[9] On the key subject of law compliance, Professor MacAvoy concluded that there is "no association between a majority of 'outside' directors and audit, nominating and compensation committees and increased law compliance."[10] With reference to corporate social responsibility, MacAvoy's empirical study "failed to show a significant difference between companies with board characteristics like the ALI and those without."[11]

On reflection, these findings comport with common sense. Independent directors are by definition divorced from any material interest in the fortunes of the corporation they oversee. Their passions and occupations are elsewhere—in other corporations or law firms or universities. They have no economic incentives to make the corporation a success. No surer mechanism could be crafted to minimize managerial drive than the system of independent directors. They probably on balance would wish for corporate success, but not with half the passion of senior management whose working life and compensation depends upon the success of the business.

It follows that independent directors will be most disposed to protect their reputation by pleasing government regulators and private do-good reform groups. They will be more likely to seek approbation of the antibusiness press or the university than would senior management who have a direct interest in maximizing corporate production and profits. The independent directors, in short, will be more willing to trade off efficiency for a good image among critics of the corporation than would management. Efficiency, in this sense, means satisfaction of consumer demand.

Furthermore, independent directors will always tend to be inefficient disciplinarians of incompetent management. They are by definition part-time directors, busy elsewhere with other concerns. That fact in conjunction with their less than burning interest in profits makes them less than ideal monitors of inefficiency in the corporation. They will always make the worst monitors for shareholders because they have no residual interest in the profits of the corporation. They therefore have no drive to be efficient monitors.

Ironically, the independent board might prove likely to enhance the power of the chief executive officer over that of the rest of the senior management. In a management-dominated board the senior management can dismiss a CEO who is incompetent. Since each management director has the same vote as the CEO, a coalition of senior vice-presidents who are on the board can purge the CEO. When only the CEO is on the board, as for example was advocated by the recent chairman of the SEC, Harold Williams, the senior management has little contact with the nonmanagement directors. The outside directors will form their opinions about senior management based only on information from the CEO. In turn, the senior management learns about the nonmanagement directors only from the CEO. The CEO is therefore in an ideal position to convince the nonmanagement directors that senior management is loyal to him, and to convince the senior management that the other directors are loyal to him.[12]

Even the assumption that independent directors are independent and, therefore, dispassionate monitors of senior management is dubious. Directors under the law are charged with the responsibility of managing the corporation. Although it is true that in reality many nonmanagement directors may perform a relatively passive oversight function, that oversight role cannot be minimized. The recent SEC report on corporate governance concluded that "two-thirds of the chairmen asked to rank the three contributions of their directors consider board participation with respect to objectives, policies, strategies and plans as most important."[13] It is clear that independent directors perform some management role. They longer they are on the board, the more likely they are to take an active interest in the corporate objectives that they have endorsed. Their independence should become suspect the longer they are on the board and the more they begin to learn about the corporation. But, of course, the reformers have done no organized psychological studies of independence or of the impact on independence of corporate directorships. It is all guesswork and surmise.

It is also likely that independent directors will have a pernicious impact on corporate disclosure policies. As a result of their conservatism and lack of entrepreneurial drive, they are always likely to opt for accounting principles that understate income, overstate expenses, overplay contingent liabilities, undervalue appraised assets, and in general demand accounting policies that are overly pessimistic. In fact, the absolutely and utterly independent accountants on the SEC staff for decades demanded conservative accounting policies from corporations that most observers today agree were terribly misleading to investors.[14]

The movement for independent directors is so suspect in light of its obvious deficiencies as to raise the suspicion that the advocates have a hidden agenda to use the reform to forestall more radical changes. The independent director program is probably endorsed by a considerable segment of the business community because they know by experience that they can pretty much get their own way despite the presence of an independent board. It appears obvious that this is so because of the part-time nature of independent directors and their lack of knowledge about the business. SEC statistics show that board members meet on an average only five to eight days per year, hardly a figure to invoke respect for the monitoring function of independent directors.[15] On the other hand, if independent directors spend more and more time at the corporation in an effort to monitor management more effectively, they will inevitably lose their independence and become more like inside management directors. It is a classic Catch-22 situation: independence requires remoteness from the business; acquisition of knowledge and expertise requires a loss of the virginal qualities of independence. Of course there is also the added factor that the more time independent directors spend on corporate business, the more necessary it is that their compensation be increased to make up for the time they lose in their other occupations. More compensation means less independence.

Independence is a quality that is useful for isolated discreet controversies. If a corporation or individual is involved in a dispute, it or he may wish the services of dispassionate arbiters to decide the controversy. In such instances independence will be a desired quality. It is not a desirable quality for men and women engaged in a continuous management role.

The peculiar quality about the independent director movement is that the financial statements of all publicly held corporations are audited by independent certified public accountants. The federal securities legislation requires it,[16] and even before the passage of those acts, a majority of the corporations listed on the New York Stock Exchange voluntarily retained independent certified public accountants (CPAs).[17] There would appear to be no need for another layer of independence between the management and the shareholders. In fact the independent certified public accountants have far greater incentive than so-called independent directors to monitor well and vigilantly. Independent accountants are paid well because of their reputation for independence. Indeed, they are retained principally for that very reputation. It is in that way that senior management is able to signal to shareholders that the financial books are in order and that the stewardship of the management is under scrutiny. The quid pro quo to management for this use of independent CPAs is increased demand for the shares of the corporation and a higher price for the stock. Studies by Watts and Zimmerman have demonstrated that for centuries before the institution of the securities acts, senior management *voluntarily retained independent accountants* because of the value of that independence.[18] Consequently the accountants have a tremendous interest in maintaining their independence and making it crystal clear to management and shareholders that they are in truth independent. The slightest hint of serious scandal will damage the reputation of a CPA firm and destroy its commercial viability. Independent directors, unlike CPAs, do not make their livelihood by force of a reputation for independence. Their principal occupation is in other ventures, not the corporation they direct. If they are thought not to be independent they lose little income compared to the remuneration they receive from their other and more important occupations. The thought then that the independence of CPAs as a general institutional pattern is in some way suspect and must be buttressed by the vigilance of independent directors is absurd.

The danger in the independent director movement is that the business community may actually begin to believe this silly stuff. More particularly, business leaders as well as academic reformers have been selling the independent director concept based upon the ludicrous thesis that has again and again been criticized in this book: that the corporation is a ministate run by powerful control groups. As I have demonstrated, the senior management is curbed by the forces of the free market that were described in Part III. Once the public mistakenly believes, however, that the modern corporation is unlimited by free-market forces, it will be a stupid public indeed that limits its reforms to the independent director idea. The thought that six or seven business executives can put on the hat called independent director, and over the course of several days per year effectively monitor the actions of senior management of a large corporation in which they have little financial interest is absurd. Although the purpose of business leaders may be to gain immunity from the attack of more radical reformers by swathing themselves in the respectability of independent directors, they will fail miserably. The independent director concept is a thin reed for the corporate community to rely on and not worth the great effort that is being put into it by such groups as the Business Roundtable, the American Law Institute, the New York Stock Exchange, and the commissioners of the SEC.

This is not to say that corporations should not, if they desire, place a few independent directors on their board. Independent directors can play useful roles. For example, a finance expert in her capacity as independent director can bring needed expertise to board deliberations. A prominent academic in the field of science or economics can assist the corporation in many problems that come before the board. A group of independent directors can evaluate proposed transactions, particularly those involving the self-interests of managerial directors, and render helpful reports.

Ironically, the SEC has recently begun to worry about the independent director ploy. Astute corporate counsel are turning increasingly to independent directors to insulate major corporate transactions from some shareholders suits. One avenue is to put the question of a derivative suit against management directors before a committee of disinterested directors. Such a derivative suit is one in which a minority shareholder compels the corporation in effect to sue a director who has allegedly harmed the corporation. If such a committee decides that the corporation should not pursue the suit, many courts will abide by the decision and dismiss the shareholder derivative suit. The court will reason that the corporation through its independent directors has exercised its business judgment that the suit will be too costly in terms of time, money, and publicity.[19] In other cases counsel will place a corporate transaction for a vote before disinterested directors. If they approve, shareholders will find it difficult to convince a court that the board has violated its duty of loyalty to shareholders. As is so usual with legal reform efforts, the proponents can seldom gauge the unexpected side effects.

Some courts have objected to the use of independent directors for ending derivative suits. They have argued that such directors can never be trusted to be truly independent of management.[20] The conclusion is ironic because it is only in such isolated transactions (as distinguished from a management role) that independent directors can be in any real sense useful to the corporation. As we have demonstrated, it is unlikely that independent directors can be effective business managers or overseers. They lack entrepreneurial drive and sufficient knowledge of the business. They can be useful, however, in judging isolated disputes such as a proposed derivative suit against certain members of management. In such a case, they can study an isolated dispute and render a judgment relatively free of self-involvement in the proposed suit. Those courts that have refused to defer to such judgments have done so on the basis that independent directors cannot ever be really independent of management control. If that judicial approach becomes widespread, independent directors will lose considerable value to management since they will never be effective in insulating corporate transactions involving management from judicial review. Such a judicial approach presages the end of the independent director reform movement.

The movement for independent directors illustrates another fundamental ailment of the SEC and the corporate and academic reformist community: the total failure adequately to develop organized scientific evidence and data supporting changes in the law. There is no evidence that independent directors manage well. In fact there is evidence that inside boards do better than outside boards. The SEC and the American Law Institute would do well to defer their propaganda attacks on management directors and instead, since they are so vitally interested in the subject, fund empirical research into the question.

The switch to boards dominated by independent directors paradoxically promises either no change or change for the worse.

It is entirely possible that independent directors may act as convenient figureheads for the CEO and/or senior management. On the other hand, to the extent that real changes result, they will be for the worse: The net result may be both public distrust of corporations and corporations saddled with disinterested directors who will be less interested than management in profits and the preservation and growth of corporate capital. In any event, as is usual with more legalistic reforms, it is likely that the implications of the changes, if any, will confound the expectations of the reformers.

10

Composition of the Board: Independent Directors and the Committee System

AUDIT COMMITTEES

Even the casual observer cannot visit the corporate scene without being struck by the emphasis on the relationship between certain key boards of directors' committees and the role of independent directors. The almost fetishistic belief in the corporate board committee structure requires some explanation. The evocation of board committees as a cure for asserted lack of corporate accountability has assumed almost a talismanic quality. One of the three magical committees is the audit committee. The functions and purpose of this entity have been described by the Securities and Exchange Commission as follows: "The first function . . . is to recommend (or approve) the . . . independent auditor."[1] This is the task of most importance since it gives the committee basic control over the employment and firing of the auditor. "The second principal function cited by most commentators is the review of the place or scope of the audit."[2] "The third . . . [function] is to

Material in this chapter is taken with changes from Nicholas Wolfson, "SEC Thinking About Corporate Governance and Accountability: Lessons in Bureaucratizing the Entrepreneurial Corporation," in *Corporate Governance: Past and Future,* pp. 12–19. Copyright © 1982 by KCG Productions, Inc. Reprinted by permission.

review the results of the annual audit, as well as the report of audit and the accompanying management letter, if any.''[3] Other important functions include ''reviewing the adequacy of internal controls''[4] and ''increased attention to the internal audit function.''[5] The SEC report further points out that audit committees are ''the most established and clearly defined of all board committees'' required by the New York Stock Exchange, ''there also is general consensus that audit committees should be composed solely of directors with no other relationship to the company.''[6]

Publicly held corporations all retain independent certified public accountants.[7] The purpose, naturally, is to establish an outside monitor of the stewardship of management. Many large publicly held corporations voluntarily retained independent CPAs even before the passage of the securities acts required it in order to inspire confidence in investors.[8] In the modern wisdom, however, one monitor is not enough. Hence the contemporary movement to establish audit committees made up exclusively of independent directors. But when you think about it, what is so crucial about one more monitoring tier? There is no empirical evidence that the second tier creates more efficiency or more honesty. If a second tier is so remarkable, why not a third tier comprised of independent accounting professors who would monitor the audit committees? In another decade this may well come to pass, or the corporate reformers will have nothing to do in the 1990s.

As I have mentioned, perhaps the most important function of the independent audit committee is control over the hiring and firing of the independent CPAs. The argument essentially is as follows: Independent accountants are not really independent if they are hired or fired by the management or by directors controlled by the management. Management will dictate accounting approaches that make them look good or in some way benefit their interests—not the shareholders'. CPA firms will follow their orders in order to retain their lucrative positions. Therefore, the external audit function must be controlled by independent audit committees. As the SEC report asserts, ''Commentators, as well as the Commission have suggested that '[t]he Audit Committee must control all services performed, and the fees received, by the auditors to insure that they are truly independent of management.''''[9]

The SEC's position illustrates the tendency described throughout this book to use totally unsubstantiated factual assertions as a basis for gradually emasculating the powers of management. There is nothing but occasional newspaper anecdotal evidence for placing control over the retention and hiring of independent CPAs exclusively in the hands of independent directors. There is absolutely no scientifically gathered evidence that management is less honest than independent directors. I continually emphasize the anecdotal nature of the basis for the corporate reform movement because it is the absence of data that acts as the great solvent with which the liberal reformers continually move to dissolve the powers of management.[10] The paradigm of the argument is monotonous and deadly. First, there is the assumption of fact—for example, that management forces CPAs to play games with accounting data. If you ask where is the data, the liberal reformers will first assert, "Well, I read about such and such scandal in the *Wall Street Journal* yesterday." When you answer that anecdotal evidence is hardly sufficient for action, they will then assert, first, that it is impossible to do scientific studies on such complex data, and second—and this is the rub for management—the burden is on management to prove its honesty, not on the academic reformers to prove their dishonesty.

In fact, as I pointed out previously, the CPA firms, as Watts and Zimmerman proved in a recent paper, have powerful incentives to remain independent.[11] They are paid, and paid well, for their reputation for integrity and independence. Independent directors, as we have said previously, do not have such incentives. They have a legal responsibility to oversee important operations of the business. They have far more reason to identify with the corporation than do the independent CPA firms. It is most likely that independent directors on audit committees will view the failure or successes of the corporation, as does management, as their responsibility. Independent-dominated audit committees are, I submit, less likely to be independent of management than are the independent CPA firms.

The point to underline is that the liberal reformers have made absolutely no studies of the psychological dynamics of independence and the independent director. Can and will an individual member of an audit committee that meets a few days a year effectively monitor CPAs? On the other hand, if he invests a great deal of time on the committee and the board, and is a member of the board for many years, can he view the work of management and the data as dispassionately as does the CPA who comes

in periodically for an audit? Will he soon identify with the corporation as does management?

But now I come to an even more fundamental point. Let us
assume with the SEC and the reformers that members of audit
committees will be independent and passionless computer monitors of management. There is every reason to believe, as we
observed in the last chapter, that they will create modes of
disclosure that will obfuscate rather than inform. Independent
directors will tend to be more conservative and less entrepreneurial than management. They will tend to demand accounting principles that underplay income, overstate expenses,
overplay contingent liabilities, undervalue appraised values,
undervalue assets, and in general always make accounting
judgments that are pessimistic and bearish.[12]

One of the principal purposes of independent director-
dominated audit committees is to prevent misrepresentation in
financial statements. Such misrepresentation may be effected by
selecting certain accounting procedures rather than others—for
example, moving from first-in-first-out (FIFO) to last-in-first-out
(LIFO) inventory accounting. Yet, Benston has pointed out that
investors are far more successful in unmasking manipulations of
accounting data than is commonly believed. He refers to studies
that demonstrate that changes in accounting procedures have little effect on stock prices; that is, investors see through the
changes.[13]

NOMINATING COMMITTEES

The general practice is for boards of directors to nominate their
successors. As we have discussed previously, management,
through its control over the proxy machinery, will see to it that
shareholders elect management-designated successor nominees.

The staff of the Securities and Exchange Commission in the
past has supported the idea that nominating committees of the
board should be established composed exclusively, or at least
largely, of independent directors in order to "facilitate [mean-
ingful] shareholder participation in the corporate electoral process."[14] The SEC staff has added a rather ominous warning that
it might recommend *direct* shareholder participation in the nomination process *rule* if nominating committees did not adequately

impound shareholder input.[15] Thus independent directors would be used to facilitate small shareholder input into the nominating process.

It is a basic truism in corporate law that each share has one vote, rather than one shareholder one vote. This is based upon the elementary fact that substantial investors will not place their capital at the disposal of small investors. The SEC, however, and the various reform groups have never quite reconciled themselves to this fact of life. Smaller shareholders are more intelligent than the SEC gives them credit for being and do not complain about their small vote since they value more the ability to sell out in efficient capital markets when the price of their stock begins to drop. Because the SEC cannot understand this calculated indifference to the vote, it continually takes steps to force management to maximize the power of *small* shareholders over the board despite shareholder indifference and the costs that the regulations entail. The Commission engages in a form of market egalitarianism designed to increase small-shareholder power beyond what it would achieve based upon its economic power. The SEC shareholder proposal rule already on the books is an example: it forces corporations to transmit shareholder proposals at corporate expense despite the minute size of the individual holdings.[16] Another example, even more dangerous, is the threat of the SEC staff to pass a rule facilitating direct shareholder nominations of directors at corporate expense on behalf of relatively small stockholders.[17] This all stems from the already described deep-seated assumption of some at the SEC that the corporation is a polity and thus the desirability of taking steps that indirectly accomplish the effect of "one person, one vote." Nothing could be more destructive of corporate efficiency than directly or indirectly changing the corporate vote from "one share, one vote" to "one shareholder, one vote." Of course, the SEC's current philosophy and rule proposals do not currently move as far as that extreme. Furthermore, the current Commission, as this book goes to press, appears to be more realistic than prior Commissions. The basic sympathy and future institutional tendency of the SEC's professional staff, however, is in that philosophical direction. The previously mentioned SEC threat to pass a rule requiring corporations to facilitate direct shareholder nomination of directors is likely to take the form one day of permitting a relatively small number of shareholders—say between one hundred and five hundred—

holding a small amount of stock each, to nominate a directorial slate. The corporate treasury would cover the costs of circulating proxy material advertising that slate.

Here, as elsewhere, reformers make recommendations without the slightest attention to economic consequences. If small shareholders are given, via governmental compulsion, greater power over the corporation than their economic clout would otherwise give them, that will lessen the incentive of large investors to place their capital in such corporations. Given the mechanisms of the efficient market, that will mean that the price of shares will drop and/or large investors will move out of the market and into more manageable investments.[18] Large and powerful shareholder groups do not need SEC intervention. They can influence boards or change management without government intervention. The SEC is not content with this, since it eliminates its function. Hence its preoccupation with small shareholders.

Another purpose of nominating committees dominated by independent directors is to maintain the separation between the board and senior management. The nominating committee would supposedly preserve control of independent directors over the nomination process and curb or dilute the control that senior management currently has over the directorial nomination process. We have already demonstrated the fallacies and weaknesses in the arguments for independent director control. This last function of the nominating committee, therefore, needs no further critical analysis in addition to that already developed here and in Chapter 9.

COMPENSATION COMMITTEES

The recent SEC report concludes that the "second most frequently cited 'oversight committee' is the compensation committee."[19] This committee sets or approves the salary of the chief executive officer and other senior management, administers stock option plans, considers "the appropriateness of compensation policies,"[20] and approves or recommends "compensation plans in which officers may participate."[21] Many commentators suggest that the compensation committee should consist exclusively of independent directors.

The goal obviously is the independent monitoring of the compensation of senior management who would otherwise, it is feared, pay themselves more than they are worth. The other purpose is to protect senior management remuneration from successful duty of loyalty litigation that—absent the committee—could attack pay packages on the ground that the management's conflict of interest invalidates the salary package.[22] The latter purpose is a valid reason, from management's vantage point, to establish such a committee. The formation of the committee is a reasonable response to the threat of vexatious litigation; as such I value it for easing the pressure on corporations from the likes of the SEC and antagonistic critics of the corporate structure. I seriously doubt, however, that independent compensation committees measure management services more effectively than would management directors.

CONCLUSION

In short, the entire independent director committee movement is a waste of energy, although for some reason it is attracting the attention of intelligent people. As a matter of fact, I believe that down deep they know it. The real hidden agenda of the independent director movement is to stave off more radical change by convincing the politicians and the public that independent directors are a reformer's panacea. The argument won't hold, however, since it is based upon the assumption that the competitive forces of the free market do not adequately curb management but that independent directors will. As I have emphasized in this book, the competitive powers of the free market do curb management and do so far more effectively than independent directors or regulation. If the public and the legislators believe that the free market is not working, they will not long be bemused by independent audit committees and independent directors. If indeed large corporations have quasi-monopolistic powers over market and products, which I don't believe the evidence establishes, then the assumption that small elite groups of "elder statesmen," called independent directors, will control such powerful forces, will not long withstand criticism. Down the road are government directors, government auditors, and government-mandated constituency directors, that is, directors who represent specific groups in society such as local communities and labor unions. The ALI and SEC philosophy; which downplays the competitive market-place, is a trap and a snare. The danger for some in the business leadership is that by endorsing the assumptions of the SEC and the academic critics about the lack of competitive forces, they will find it impossible in the end to justify the current status quo. Step by step in future years they, along with an enthusiastic govern-ment, will be driven by the inexorable logic of their position to move more and more in the direction of transforming the modern efficient corporation into an arm not of enlightened management or even of independent directors, but of the government.

11

Composition of the Board: Labor Directors

DURING THE PAST TWO DECADES the leaders of Western Europe have become supporters of the concept of labor representation on the boards of directors. Pursuant to a system called codetermination, labor is granted 50 percent, in certain cases, of the governing board of directors. The philosophy of "industrial democracy" has received a cool reception from American labor unions, which to date have been satisfied with the power they have in the collective bargaining process. Although there are some limited exceptions, as in the recent case of Chrysler where the union received a seat on the board, the approach even in the sense of minority representation has not been followed in the United States.

According to Furubotn, the pratice of codetermination in Europe has had only a modest effect on the practices of industrial concerns.[1] Management has apparently preserved its powers while observing the forms of "industrial democracy." The future ramifications are, however, quite serious and threaten the ultimate demise of the free-market corporate system as we know it. In this chapter I rely on and summarize the work of Furubotn, who has studied this system in great detail.[2]

Labor directors can be expected to focus on two dimensions of the corporation: the working environment and wages. In the free enterprise corporate structure workers have a choice of corporations in which to work. They can, depending upon their individual preferences, work at a shop that pays high wages but provides an unpleasant or dangerous work place due to the nature of the product being manufactured. They can, if they prefer, trade off wages for a pleasant and restful work place at another corporation. Workers and corporations will bargain with each other and an equilibrium will be reached in which, within certain limits, workers' individual utility preferences match corporate wage and environmental offers. As Furubotn put it, ''Profit-maximizing firms and utility-maximizing workers use contracts and markets to achieve a system-wide equilibrium in which each firm maintains the 'quality' of its production environment at the highest level permitted by existing technology, current market prices, and the willingness of workers to substitute nonpecuniary for pecuniary rewards.''[3]

Now assume that corporations are dominated by labor boards and make the further assumption that the labor boards do not demand fundamental income redistribution in favor of workers. Instead assume they demand a better working environment in return for lower cash wages. This will penalize those individuals who would have chosen otherwise. They are now forced to work in a firm for lower wages than they would otherwise have sought.[4] Furthermore, the productive efficiency of many firms will decline and prices will rise for consumers. As Furubotn suggests, consider a noisy boiler factory. Efforts to reduce the noise level in that kind of plant may enormously raise costs of production. The result will ultimately be a lower package of wages, a poorer working environment, and a chill on employment because of the high cost of the plant.[5]

In the free enterprise corporate system, however, workers are free to move from one corporation to the next in search of a trade off between wages and working conditions that will best satisfy their individual preference. Those workers who want easier working conditions at lower wages will be able to find a plant, let us say a perfume factory, in which the environment can be made pleasant at less cost to the firm than would be the case for the boiler factory. That is, in a free enterprise system management creates an environment that is consistent with the exigencies of the competitive system. A boiler factory is noisy. To make it less noisy will render it inefficient. However, workers are free to choose to work instead in the perfume factory. In labor-dominated corporations, both the boiler plant and the perfume factory will have a "sweet" environment plus low wages; but the boiler factory will also be so inefficient as a result, that workers there will end up with lower total rewards than they would in a free-market system, where they are free to choose to work in a perfume factory and leave the boiler factory to workers who prefer high cash wages to a quiet environment.

On the other hand it may be argued that labor-dominated firms will compete vigorously and that because of the different preferences of workers at different plants, each labor-dominated firm will offer to peripatetic workers a varied mix of trade-offs between working environment and cash wages. At that point, however, the new labor system will merely begin to *mimic* the current working of the free enterprise corporate system. It will not be better. Furthermore, the assumption that such firms will compete is unlikely. Labor unions are likely to dictate uniform trade-offs across the whole of a given industry and probably across different industries. The choices will be political and workers in the minority will be coerced. Of course the example also works if labor chooses higher cash wages over pleasant environment. Workers will be worse off, or at best will perhaps approach the present system.

The foregoing discussion assumes that labor-dominated boards will not demand a radical redistribution of corporate wealth. This is an unlikely suggestion. Labor representatives will have a shorter time perspective than equity owners of the corporation. They will opt for a *greater total benefit package now,* since it is to their advantage to take as much as they can extract during their working lives and to hell with what happens afterward. The shareholders of corporations and managers with equity interests in the business are interested in the long run. The principal reason is their equity interest. If the corporation is perceived as successfully planning for the long run, their equity interest will increase in value. Therefore, they have a present interest in responsible long-run planning, including moderate corporate wage policies. Furthermore, senior management tends to be sensitive to the value of their equity interest in the corporation for the benefit of their children and spouses and their retirement years. As a result, senior management coordinates and administers the various inputs—including labor—with a view to optimizing the profits of the concern *over the long run.*

This explanation becomes even more convincing when we consider the operations of the efficient market for shares. If senior management under labor board domination begins to allocate a greater amount to labor than the competitive market for labor warrants, the price of their corporate shares will drop significantly relative to those of management-dominated corporations. This will mean immediate income loss to shareholders including senior management. Their ability to raise equity and debt capital will suffer. Senior management will also suffer another loss. Their ability to obtain superior income packages and better positions at other corporations will decrease since the competitive market for management will judge their wage decision harshly.

Because of the efficient market, senior management has a great incentive to coordinate efficiently the inputs and demands upon the corporation. It balances wage demands, dividend demands, demands of suppliers, so as to maximize profits. Profits are the lifeblood of liberal capitalist society. They provide the resources for new technology, expansion of the firm, and development of new businesses. Profits force firms to allocate resources in those directions that satisfy consumer preferences. The efficient market compels the senior management to perform the balancing act efficiently. If they fail, the price of the shares will drop and new management may take over by virtue of the market for control. If senior management, by design or incompetence, begins to pay out too much in dividends, then equity capital will flow into corporations that have struck a wiser balance. The same thing happens if management pays out too much in wages.

In conclusion, in an industry where some firms are labor-dominated, but not all, capital and management will flow out of the labor firms and into the shareholder-dominated firms. Labor-dominated boards will jack up wages and fringe benefits. The efficient market will react. Prices of the shares of stock will drop. Investors will seek investments in corporations that are not labor-dominated. In the competitive race the traditional free enterprise corporations will prevail as they always have in the past in the United States. No voluntary labor-dominated enterprise of any great size has been started and become successful, although there is no law against labor starting a corporation anywhere in the

United States. New capital will not be invested in labor concerns. Shareholders who have already invested in a labor-dominated corporation will sell in an effort to get out of a business that offers them much less in the way of dividends. Lenders will be reluctant to advance loan capital to those concerns, since the interest of labor is to obtain short-run wage increases at the price of the long-run viability of concerns. Although such corporations will be able to raise some capital by retaining earnings, it will be significantly less than in the current structure. *Therefore government will have to force all of industry to be subject to labor-dominated boards if it wishes to preserve labor-dominated corporations.*

Now let us pursue this scenario further. *Assume that all industries are dominated by labor boards that wish to redistribute wealth to labor.* At this juncture the shareholders still exist and the stock markets are still functioning since industry has not yet been nationalized. Capital will avoid industries that are redistributing wealth. Shareholders will sell and look for alternative investments. Senior management will leave corporations and search for alternative opportunities not dominated by labor unions. If the economy remains free, shareholders and management may be able to establish new industries that are still free of labor boards. If that is forbidden by law, capital will continue to flow out of all industry and move into luxury consumptions. Investors will prefer the purchase of yachts and Rolls Royces to equity investments that return little or nothing or that have negative returns. While this is going on there will be great disruption and near panic in the stock markets. It seems inevitable that at some point government will step in to prevent the flight of capital by law and regulation. But that doesn't solve the problem of obtaining new capital. Corporations will have to proceed with less capital and less industrial research and technology. Prices will rise for consumers. Employment will drop. The government—not private investors—will be forced to act as the source of capital. Government will not do that unless it can exercise control. A socialized economy will be the inevitable end result.

A further problem will arise. Each labor union will have interests that conflict with the economy and the general public. For example the labor unions that dominate the steel industry will increase wages to as high a level as they dare. It is in their interest to do so since they are not equity holders with a stake in the long-term future of the industry. Their time span is the twnenty or so years they plan to work before retiring. Steel prices will therefore rise. The interests of the steel union workers will conflict with industries and consumers that purchase steel. The disciplining mechanism of the capital markets will have been damaged or destroyed. The government will have to step in and regulate wages and ultimately prices of steel. A statist economy will inevitably result.

12

Some Final Notes on the Role of the Board of Directors

It now remains to develop a modern theory of the board of directors. Actually the task has already been accomplished. The modern theory of the firm discussed in Chapter 4, Chapters 9–11 on independent and labor directors, and Chapter 5 on markets for control have articulated such a theory. This chapter need only assemble the parts.

State law provides that directors have the power and responsibility to manage the corporation. Many statutes have been amended in the recent past to provide that corporations shall be managed by *or under the direction of* the board. The phrase "under the direction" was intended to make clear that directors of large corporations could delegate managerial duty to officers of the corporation. Under the statute, however, the ultimate responsibility remains with the board which is the supreme managerial institution of the corporation. Recent articles and speeches by business school professors, lawyers, and businessmen have disputed this legal assumption. The popular theory today is that directors do not manage. It is argued that boards of directors should be *monitors* of the management efforts of senior management. Boards, in other words, exist to evaluate the financial, business, and legal ramifications of the decisions of senior management. Directors are presumed to be apart from, and in some sense in conflict with, or antagonistic to, senior management. Management proposes and disposes; but if the effects are less than satisfactory—for example, if profits drop significantly, or significant laws are broken—the board sits in judgment and reproves or even removes the management.

The current theory, it is clear, depends upon the *predominance* of independent directors. If a board is exclusively a management board, the monitoring function becomes an absurdity in the absolutist sense preached by its proponents.

In an earlier chapter I described and analyzed the failure and fallacies of the independent director concept. I have also analyzed fallacies of the so-called shareholder democracy approach pursuant to which small shareholders would select and elect independent directors. I have also set forth the powerful disciplinary functions of the markets for control and management. In the light of those facts a true picture of the ideal board of directors emerges. The board is a management group that specializes in coordinating the various inputs into the corporation such as labor, capital, supplies, and the like.[1] The directors (who are also the senior management) coordinate these inputs with the purpose of maximizing return to the risk-takers or shareholders. I have pointed out how senior management is a specialist in monitoring inputs. It monitors well because of its interest in profits, and the market for management and control. But ironically there is no need at this juncture in the analysis to have something called a board, as distinguished from senior management, if we accept the idea that independent directors need not and should not dominate the board. A board made up exclusively or principally of senior management *is* senior management. Indeed, those persons who would act as independent directors, as long as they are not in control, need not be directors. The senior management could obtain their advice as consultants. Why then have something called a board of directors? The answer lies in the importance of the market for control and occasionally the proxy battlefield. *A legal method must be delineated by which incompetent senior management can be displaced. The process that accomplishes this relies on (a) the vote for directors that attaches to common stock, and (b) the institution of the board of directors. Rival management groups can displace incompetent managers by buying stock, taking control of the board, and using board power to fire incompetents. This can and is done most effectively by the market for control and particularly the stock or cash take-over route. Sometimes the proxy route can be effectively used. In that process lies the real and only relevance of the board institution.*

The role of the board fits in with the theory of the firm outlined in Chapter 4. Senior management in the corporation specializes in monitoring the shirking of inputs to the corporation. It monitors junior management. It supervises labor. It seeks out new capital at the best possible rates. But who monitors the monitor? By now the answer is clear: the markets for product, control, and management. The markets for control and management need a legal mechanism. That modality is *the common stock vote and the board.*

PART V

SEC Regulation of Corporations: The Failure of Federal Regulation

13

The Failures of the Securities and Exchange Commission

INTRODUCTION

No examination of the corporation is complete without an analysis of the Securities and Exchange Commission (SEC), the federal agency that regulates the American corporation. Just as we have examined state judicial doctrine and state corporate statutes, we must also explore the philosophical and empirical underpinning of federal regulation of the corporation. We must determine whether proper corporate theory justifies or, on the contrary, condemns the regulatory structure of the SEC.

The SEC is fifty years old as this book goes to press.[1] This famous agency is no longer a regulatory stripling. Middle age has set in and the uninitiated might believe that the SEC has lost its youthful vigor. They would be wrong, for in recent years, the SEC has proved its continuing strength and energy, producing a veritable mountain of new and proposed regulations and forms.[2] Meanwhile, the massive new Federal Securities Code, or more likely parts of it, sponsored by the American Law Institute, may possibly be introduced in Congress.[3] This proposed legislation, drafted by an experienced group of prestigious lawyers, would grant significant new regulatory power to the SEC.[4] No economists, however, were part of the drafting process and no economic empirical research was utilized to measure costs and benefits of the proposed new Code.[5] Now that the SEC has achieved the half century mark, it is time to critically measure the successes and failures of the agency and the laws it administers.

In the past the SEC has rarely engaged in any empirical studies to determine whether current or proposed regulations are necessary to decrease abuses in the securities industry. Furthermore, the SEC typically fails to evaluate whether the benefits of current or proposed regulations outweigh the burdens imposed on the industry. The purpose of Part V of this book is to examine the efficacy of the regulatory scheme as enforced by the SEC. I explore the 1930s and modern economic theories of the corporation to determine whether any support exists for the current regulatory scheme. Next, certain programs of the SEC are analyzed. The major emphases of Part V are (a) to promote a critical examination of the need for SEC regulation, (b) to illustrate the necessity for future empirical research, and (c) to demonstrate the advantages of free-market constraints as compared to SEC regulation.

SEC REGULATORY THEORY FAILS BOTH LIBERAL AND CONSERVATIVE CRITERIA

Modern Conservative and Liberal
Philosophy of Regulation

The federal government has recently been successful in deregulating the trucking[6] and airline industries,[7] and in enacting legislation prohibiting state fair-trade laws.[8] Many of these endeavors succeeded because of the formation of a curious alliance between conservatives and liberals.[9] The former believed that federal agencies were unduly interfering with the operation of the free market, whereas the latter (as well as some conservatives) proceeded under the assumption that the older agencies had fallen victim to the ''iron triangle'' syndrome. According to this theory, agencies created to oversee and regulate a particular industry become the captives of (1) the regulated industry, (2) Congress and the subcommittee that has jurisdiction over the agency, and (3) the bureaucratic staff of the agency itself. Because of the strong influences exerted by the regulated industry, it is not unusual to observe the agencies turning toward the interest of business rather than providing protection for the public. Some influential analysts, including Stigler, have asserted that most government regulatory agencies were initially established as a result of lobbying by the affected industry.[10] Moreover, economists during the preceding decade have produced an impressive body of empirical research which proved in case after case that government regulation was harming rather than benefiting the public.[11] Conservative thinkers in broad outline agreed with liberals that deregulation was needed to address these problems, and were therefore willing to join with liberals in dismantling the regulation of certain affected industries.

At the same time as some deregulation was occurring, however, the Congress, with the support of some of the same liberals who had attacked the older agencies, passed a vast new body of regulation in the fields of environment, safety, transportation, and pensions, and new agencies were formed to enforce the congressional mandates. The Consumer Product Safety Commission,[12] for example, "controls the safety of virtually every consumer product on the market,"[13] the Environmental Protection Agency[14] deals with pollution problems "created by all industries,"[15] and the Occupational Safety and Health Review Commission[16] supervises "safety and health conditions for workers in all industries."[17] The dollar impact of the new regulation dwarfs that of previous regulation. The liberals, who had distrusted the old agencies, attempted to establish new approaches to ensure that business would have little or no influence in the new agencies. Because of the belief that the influence of the regulated industries had resulted in abuse, the newer legislation established agencies that cut across particular industry lines and was extremely detailed in application in an effort to force the regulators to remain hostile to the regulated interests.[18]

Liberals and conservatives alike, however, have recognized in recent years that the passage of a law will not necessarily bring about the desired result. Both sides fear or anticipate capture of the agency by the bureaucracy or the regulated interests. Liberal thinkers believe that with the right safeguards, legislation can accomplish a better result than the free workings of the marketplace. Conservative economists dispute that belief, and have frequently demonstrated the unexpected and negative results of regulation.[19]

*Securities Regulation Falls Outside Conservative
and Liberal Thinking*

The world of securities legislation appears to fall outside of both
modern liberal and conservative schools of thought. The Securities Act of 1933 (Securities Act) and the Securities Exchange Act
of 1934 (Exchange Act) were passed by legislators who held very
optimistic beliefs in the value of legislation for its own sake. Their
fundamental conviction that the benefits of legislation always exceeded the costs was such an article of faith at the time that it
assumed spiritual rather than empirical form. Enormous discretionary authority was placed in the SEC in the form of rulemaking power.[20] In case after case, the SEC was permitted to
promulgate regulations that were not only ''necessary'' but often
only ''appropriate'' to protect investors or the public from
fraudulent and misleading practices.[21] Most of the broad discretionary powers delegated by Congress were held by the attorney-
bureaucrats who dominated the SEC. The legislation, however,
also delegated enormous discretionary powers of regulation to
business groups organized as stock exchanges,[22] such as the New
York Stock Exchange, and to an over-the-counter trade association called the National Association of Securities Dealers
(NASD).[23] In turn, those business-dominated self-regulatory
agencies were to be controlled by the SEC, which had significant
discretionary power over them.[24] Modern liberals would have
great doubts about the wisdom of such a self-regulatory structure
and broad discretionary mandate. Modern free-market conservatives would be extremely skeptical about entrusting so much
discretion in the hands of government regulators and affected
business groups.

SEC REGULATION IS PRODUCED
TO SUPPLY ATTORNEY DEMAND

Attorney Demand for Regulation

The 1930s liberals who were responsible for this statutory scheme
had a much greater faith than today's liberals (and, of course,
conservatives) in the ability of the SEC to remain independent of

the bureaucracy and the private bar. That faith proved unjustified: the SEC, like many other regulatory agencies, became entangled in a symbiotic relationship with attorneys in the private securities bar. The attorneys employed by the SEC usually spent only a few years at the agency. They would then be hired by the private bar, exchanges, NASD, or corporations to interpret the regulations that they had helped pass. Therefore, they had strong motives to preserve and expand the regulatory structure that underlay their careers. The bureaucrats who remained with the agency had obvious reasons to increase their own power and responsibility. The authors of the legislation were mistaken in their belief that the regulators of the SEC would remain independent. Moreover, they also failed to recognize that the uncontrolled delegation of broad discretionary powers would result in the proliferation of regulations by SEC attorneys whose careers were dependent upon government domination of the securities industry.

The SEC has always been dominated by attorneys. Although accountants and financial analysts work for the agency and head up some of its branches or divisions, the major power bases in the agency have been occupied by attorneys.[25] The securities bar is made up of an unusually able and responsible group of professionals. Its members frequently begin their careers with the SEC because of public-spirited goals and many maintain that laudable attitude throughout their professional careers. Good intentions, however, do not ensure that the activities undertaken by these professionals will benefit the investing public. SEC attorneys make their living interpreting laws and regulations. Attorneys who seek to maximize their utility as employees, therefore, will always add to regulation rather than decrease it. Whether they are liberal or conservative, members of the Democratic or Republican party, they benefit from more rather than less regulation. This is true for the great majority who leave the agency to enter private practice as well as for the relatively smaller number who remain at the agency, since whether an attorney is promulgating regulations or interpreting them for a client, more legal work is generated.

Those few SEC attorneys in positions of power who enter the agency with a determination to decrease regulation face immense psychological pressures to change their ways. Bureaucratic rewards are based upon excellence, speed, and facility in producing new regulations. A conservative who works at the SEC will quickly realize that the work expected of him or her is the drafting of these new and additional regulations. The SEC attorney who balks at this process and produces less regulation is quickly identified as an iconoclast, or worse, an enemy of the agency espirit de corps. Her "in box" empties, she is no longer invited to meetings, and ultimately she is revealed to the press by her colleagues as an obstructionist. The activist attorney, in contrast, is admired by the press; he makes good copy. If regulators do not regulate actively the press has little to write about. A good reputation in the press as an activist is bankable. Regulated industries will pay rich salaries to SEC attorneys who develop a reputation for skill and energy.

Attorney Hostility Toward Empirical Research Maximizes the Quantity of Regulation

The attorney's ignorance of and antipathy toward organized scientific empirical research adds fuel to their self-interest in more regulation. If attorney regulators were to make a systematic effort to measure empirically the impact of proposed regulation, a significantly smaller regulatory burden would be placed upon industry. Systematic empirical research is, however, foreign to the training and experience of attorney regulators.[26] Instead they seek public and industry written responses to a rule proposal or at best a hearing at which interest groups present evidence which the agency is free to consider or ignore. Indeed, it was only in recent years that the SEC staff began to conduct organized, sophisticated studies of the empirical impact of regulations.[27]

Thus, the lack of consideration for empirical research combined with the self-interest in continued and increasing regulation means that the attorney-dominated SEC is not motivated to decrease regulation, but to increase its hold on industry. While the legal profession is benefited by the perpetual increase in paperwork and research required, it is not at all clear that regulated industries and their investors derive any benefit whatsoever.

THE FLAWED ECONOMIC THEORY
THAT UNDERLIES SEC PHILOSOPHY

The 1930s Economic Theory

As we have discussed earlier, in the early 1930s, Berle and Means, and other writers popularized the notion of the existence of a separation of ownership and control of the publicly held corporation.[28] According to this theory, the publicly held corporation was managed by a small self-perpetuating group of officers and directors who frequently had only a tiny ownership interest in the corporation. This group managed the money invested by the powerless and passive body of public shareholders. When the interests of the owners and the managers diverged, the directors could and would take action to their benefit at the expense of the shareholders. The perceived evils of separation of ownership and control were the basis for the New Deal securities legislation.[29] The New Deal Congress did not believe for one moment that the free market could be relied upon in any sense to curb unprincipled conduct by corporate insiders, whether in the sale of securities or in other activities related to management of publicly held corporations.

The response of Congress to its belief in the fundamental illegitimacy of the large publicly held American corporation was to create the SEC,[30] an agency charged with regulating the issuance and trading of corporate securities.[31] The SEC came to symbolize the need for and the value of the concept of the regulatory agency. Since the SEC was blessed not only by an apparently admirable purpose, but by a remarkable staff, its reputation soon was preeminent among the agencies of government.[32]

Modern Economic Theory

With the development of sophisticated new ways of analyzing the corporation and the market for its securities, it has become more apparent in recent years that the theory on which the creation of the SEC was based was fundamentally flawed.[33] As we have demonstrated in the earlier sections of this book, the separation of ownership and control is not some theological original corporate sin; rather, such a model is the natural and spontaneous choice of tens of thousands of shareholders who are looking for successful investment vehicles. Public shareholders do not have the time, knowledge, experience, or desire to manage corporations, whereas officers and directors are skilled in managing businesses.

Modern economic analysis of the market and the publicly held corporation presents convincing reasons for a belief in the efficacy of the forces of competition in the market to monitor the behavior of the corporation. This conclusion is reinforced by the legislative history of the federal securities acts. Conventional wisdom assumes that massive stock frauds led to the drafting and passage of the Securities Act and the Exchange Act. Benston laid that myth to rest in his analysis of legislative hearings. He pointed out that there is very little evidence to buttress the claim that the financial statements of publicly traded corporations were fraudulent in the period prior to promulgation of the securities laws. Indeed, the United States Senate hearings leading to the enactment of the Securites Act of 1933 referred to a mere handful of phony financial statements. In addition, only a scattering of judicial cases prior to 1934 accused CPAs or corporations of misleading financial statements.[34] While noting the difficulty of maintaining suits against accountants prior to the enactment of the Securities Act, Benston points out that only a handful of suits were brought until the 1960s, which indicates that there was no intent to sue accountants that was frustrated by the problem of maintaining such a suit.[35]

Benston further concluded that he found no documentation of fraudulent accounting information in prospectuses for the sale of stock in pre-1933 years, although he conceded that obviously there must have been some misrepresentation. He then pointed out that there were massive frauds after the enactment of the securities acts, such as the famous Equity Funding, Home-Stake Investments, Yale Express, and National Student Marketing cases. Indeed, he stated that it may be easier to gull investors today because the presence of the SEC convinces them that crooked, phony financial data are a problem that have been solved.[36]

With this proper economic perspective, analysis of the need for the extensive existing securities legislation and its watchdog, the SEC, assumes a different proportion. Many corporate and securities attorneys appear automatically to assume the need for legislation and government agency oversight to generate adequate corporate disclosure and eliminate massive corporate securities fraud. The preceding materials and chapters illustrate the lack of historical evidence of extensive fraud, and establish that if fraud does exist, market forces will effectively deal with it. While this conclusion does not irrefutably demonstrate the lack of efficacy of the SEC, it does indicate the need for a serious evaluation of the SEC's actual programs and actions.

THE EFFICIENT MARKET THEORY DISCREDITS SEC DISCLOSURE DOCTRINE

In recent years a considerable body of new economic research on the "efficient market," in addition to the materials developed above, has thrown into serious question SEC disclosure doctrine. It has always been taken for granted that a professional analyst who investigates the financial and business history of a corporation can predict individual future stock prices better than a naive investor who invests ignorantly without research. This cliche has been based on the assumption that the professional investor can predict the future; it assumes that there is some correlation between prior earnings, prior sales, prior success, and future performance of the corporation. But upon deeper consideration, this assumption is not so easily defended.

Questioning the Old Assumptions

To begin with, it is very difficult to predict the future. Although it is possible to discover that the stock of a corporation is undervalued because other analysts have failed to recognize the valuable characteristics of this corporation, the difficulty in doing so is that much information about the corporation is in the public domain. The most reasonable likelihood is that some analysts have recognized those characteristics and have begun to purchase the stock, thereby bidding up its price. Of course, if the information is nonpublic material, it cannot lawfully be used.

It is, therefore, very possible that the price of corporate stock at all times already reflects public evaluation of all relevant data

about the corporation. The only legitimate possibility to outperform the market is for the professional investor to evaluate public
data and predict the future in a way that nobody else in the public
has been able to do. This is not very likely, as empirical findings
have confirmed. Virtually all attempts to beat the market average
are unsuccessful except for chance and luck because stock prices
already incorporate all the information about the past and predictions of the future. Prices will change as new information is
revealed, but since nobody can predict the nature of such new information, nobody can predict the stock prices of tomorrow. The
economic doctrines described are called the "random walk" and
"efficient market" hypotheses.[37]

Numerous economic studies have shown that professional
managers are unable to outperform market averages. The attempts continue, however. Ehrbar in *Fortune* referred to Jensen's
"religious theory of the demand for security analysis":

> If investors cannot profit from security analysts' advice, why do they
> employ so many analysts? [Professor] Jensen has volunteered what
> he calls the "religious theory of the demand for security analysis."
> He suggests that investors have a very low tolerance for mysteries—
> they are uncomfortable not knowing where the price of their stocks
> are going. And so they hire people who write stories explaining the
> market much as other credulous individuals try to reduce the amount
> of mystery in their lives by turning to astrologers and gurus.[38]

As a result of these new findings, two experts in the field of
finance, Langbein and Posner,[39] assert that trustees and investment managers should no longer engage in the fruitless endeavor
of individual stock picking. They should invest in what are called
"index" or "market funds." In the words of the authors,

> "[T]hese are . . . funds that have abandoned the traditional at-
> tempt to "beat the market" by picking and choosing among
> securities. . . . Instead, they create and hold essentially unchanged
> a portfolio of securities that is designed to approximate some index
> of market performance such as the Standard & Poor's 500. The S&P
> 500 is a hypothetical portfolio consisting of 500 major nonfinancial
> companies on the New York Stock Exchange weighted by the mar-
> ket value of each company's total outstanding shares.[40]

Adverse Impact on SEC Doctrine

The consequences of the efficient market doctrine are far-reaching. They extend beyond the recommendation that proposed investment managers should turn to index funds rather than individual selection of stock.[41] Much of the brokerage industry involves the giving of advice to individuals or institutions about individual securities based on fundamental analysis of financial statements and data concerning particular firms. But brokers cannot successfully pick individual stocks. The individual or institutional investor, therefore, should invest in an index fund or get out of the market. Brokerage employees and research department personnel should be transferred to index fund development or get out of the business entirely. SEC personnel who regulate brokers and other stock advisers should retire.

Fundamental SEC and judicial doctrine on investment advice become suspect. This legal doctrine, called the "shingle theory," in essence provides that a broker "cannot recommend a security unless there is an adequate and reasonable basis for such recommendation. . . . By his recommendation he implies that a reasonable investigation has been made and that his recommendation rests on the conclusions based on such investigation."[42] This legal doctrine is the cornerstone for much of the SEC regulation of investment advisers, investment bankers, and stock brokers in their role as advisers. But if the random-walk and efficient-market thesis is correct, then no broker-dealer or adviser can rationally recommend an individual security. She can only recommend an index fund.

The broker can theoretically get around this result by disclosing to the investor that the broker's advice is worthless. At that point, presumably the investor has the right to accept and rely upon the advice known to him to be worthless.

The usefulness of SEC and other financial data about corporations is suspect under the new economic doctrine. The efficient-market and random-walk findings indicate that there is no correlation between past earnings and future earnings. Therefore, the utility of the data to the individual investor is nil.

The SEC was created in the first instance to improve the investor's ability to select individual securities. Much of SEC anti-fraud doctrine is based on that assumption. Since the efficient market eliminates the rationality of individual stock selection and the evidence we have discussed elsewhere in this book indicates that market forces will cause corporations to make adequate disclosure, the justification for the SEC is weakened.

ARBITRARY DEFINITION OF MATERIALITY

The inability of the SEC to measure the efficacy of its disclosure requirements is exacerbated by another fundamental weakness of SEC mandated disclosure—the arbitrary definition of materiality used by the agency and the courts.[43] Indeed, the inability to define clearly the concept of materiality may be the cause of the incessant flow of unnecessary regulatory changes. The concept of materiality is the foundation of mandatory disclosure. The SEC, as well as the courts, determine what must be disclosed by reference to the concept of materiality. In SEC rule 405 the SEC defines the term material as follows:

> The term "material," when used to qualify a requirement for the furnishing of any information as to any subject, limits the information required to those matters to which there is a substantial likelihood that a reasonable investor would attach importance in determining whether to purchase the security registered.[44]

The federal courts have addressed the same concept. In *SEC* v. *Texas Gulf Sulphur Co.*,[45] the court defined the term in the following manner: "The basic test of materiality . . . is whether a *reasonable man* would attach importance . . . in determining his choice of action."[46] The court went on to state that this "encompasses any fact . . . which in reasonable and objective contemplation *might* affect the value of the corporation's stock or securities."[47]

In *TSC Industries, Inc.* v. *Northway, Inc.*,[48] the Supreme Court rendered a decision in the proxy regulation context which probably now applies across the board to define materiality in all SEC contexts. The Court defined materiality in the following manner:

> An omitted fact is material if there is a *substantial likelihood* that a reasonable shareholder would consider it important in deciding how to vote. This standard is fully consistent with *Mills'* general description of materiality as a requirement that 'the defect have a significant *propensity* to affect the voting process.' It does not require proof of a substantial likelihood that disclosure of the omitted fact would

have caused the reasonable investor to change his vote. What the standard does contemplate is a showing of a substantial likelihood that, under all the circumstances, the omitted fact would have assumed *actual significance* in the deliberations of the reasonable shareholder. Put another way, there must be a substantial likelihood that the disclosure of the omitted fact would have been viewed by the reasonable investor as having *significantly altered* the ''total mix'' of information made available. [Emphasis added.][49]

The importance of the concept is obvious but in reality it is difficult to apply. Clearly, a mistake in a zip code is not a material disclosure error for a corporate issuer. Failure to mention the major destruction of a plant is a material disclosure error. It is the cases in between the extremes that are hard to characterize. The SEC and the courts use key verbal formulae such as ''would'' or ''might'' or ''substantially affect'' or ''average prudent investor.'' Clearly, a rational basis for developing a more precise definition exists. Materiality for the investor, as distinguished perhaps from the creditor, has some connection to the future price of the stock. A fact, opinion, or prediction is material if its revelation will have a statistically significant impact on the price of the security. A materially bullish fact is important to the investor because knowing that fact, a significant number of investors are more likely to hold or buy. A materially bearish fact likewise is significant because possession of it will incline or cause investors to sell. Unless an empirical, as distinguished from verbal, formula can be established, the SEC and the courts will succeed only in fabricating administrative or judicial fiat rather than establishing meaningful criteria which will assist issuers in conforming their conduct to a mandated standard.

Economists and accountants have engaged in empirical studies to establish the meaning of materiality.[50] The accounting profession has been engaged for some years in an effort to establish a rational basis for disclosure.[51] The SEC, however, has refrained from systematic and comprehensive empirical studies to define materiality with reference to its numerous mandated disclosure requirements,[52] taking instead an approach similar to one of the holdings in a famous disclosure case. In *Escott* v. *Barchris Construction Company,*[53] the judge as fact-finder determined that the corporation in question had overstated earnings per share by some 14 percent. The corporation also had overstated current assets and understated current liabilities. The judge quoted an early SEC decision, In the Matter of Charles A. Howard,[54] which defined a material fact as "a fact which if it had been correctly stated or disclosed would have deterred or tended to deter the average prudent investor from purchasing the securities in question."[55] He then stated:

> Since no one knows what moves or does not move the mythical "average prudent investor," it comes down to a question of judgment, to be exercised by the trier of the fact as best he can in the light of all the circumstances. It is my best judgment that the average prudent investor would not have cared about these errors in the 1960 sales and earnings figures, regrettable though they may be. I therefore find that they were not material within the meaning of Section 11.[56]

That arbitrary approach has been the standard of the SEC and the courts. They both adhere to verbal formulas which may or may not have a real world connection to materiality. An agency and judiciary which have no firm grasp of the concept of materiality will create, mandate, and administer a meaningless disclosure policy. Since the SEC has conducted no program to validate empirically its many mandatory disclosure items, it is difficult to understand how the SEC disclosure policy could serve any useful function for the securities market.

CONCLUSION

Modern economic analysis has gravely weakened, if not irretrievably damaged, the theoretical basis for the mandatory disclosure system of securities legislation enforced by the SEC. Even if it is assumed that some mandatory disclosure is necessary, any fair-minded observer must at the least recognize that the rationalization for the system is so dubious that the burden of proving the need for a regulatory structure, or any part of it, has shifted from the critics to the supporters of the system. To change the burden in practice is extremely difficult, however, because the administrators and implementors of the system are principally members of the securities bar who have been educated, trained, and suitably rewarded to accept the fundamental vagaries of the regulatory system. The essential goal at the SEC and the private securities bar is to polish and refine the existing system. Any disposition by the private bar to question the structure is discouraged by SEC policies which are directed to an effort to co-opt the private bar into an enforcement auxiliary of the agency. Hope for regulatory reform must lie with an effort by the executive branch to introduce into the SEC administration significant numbers of persons who are tough-minded deregulators. Otherwise, the chance of any real reform will be miniscule.[57]

14

Lack of Empirical Basis for SEC Regulation: Some Case Studies

INTRODUCTION

In the main, federal securities laws are based on unproven assumptions that they will achieve their purposes, rather than on empirical proof that they will do so. A securities law or a regulation promulgated by the Securities and Exchange Commission typically is founded on untested beliefs about its effectiveness. Even scholarly legal literature in the field of securities law is occupied almost exclusively with problems of interpreting the language of the statutes and cases instead of the more important, but much more difficult, problem of empirically testing the actual utility of the law.[1] The best that can be said for the current scheme is that securities laws are usually based on common sense intuitions about a regulation's real effect on market performance and investor behavior. But common sense by itself is inadequate to evaluate the enormously complicated structure and dynamics of securities regulation. This chapter briefly identifies the need for empirical research, using as an example the ''private offering'' exemption from the registration provisions of the Securities Act of 1933.

The Deficiencies of the Traditional Approach

The following developmental pattern typifies the history of the ordinary securities law or regulation. First, there is an *unproven assumption of fact:* for example, that securities prospectuses assist investor decision making. Next there is the legal follow-through on this assumption in the form of a *regulation, judicial pronouncement, or statute:* the SEC promulgates prospectus regulations and disclosure guides.[2] The regulations, pronouncements, and statutes then require *interpretation,*[3] a function performed by courts and legions of attorneys. Interpretation of a regulation is concerned with its applicability to specific factual situations in the securities markets. After the promulgation and interpretation of a rule, legal academicians engage in *traditional legal scholarship,* which involves the production of articles criticizing interpretations X, Y, and Z, and recommending alternative interpretations A, B, and C. Often these articles merely analyze the words of the law or point out its inconsistency with other laws. Significantly, these reformulations are based on assumptions as devoid of empirical basis as the original rule.

Thus a securities rule is promulgated, interpreted, applied, and evaluated without any evidence about the effectiveness of the rule in the market. Societal goals can be best effectuated through such a lawmaking process only if the assumption on which the legal rule is based is correct. For example, empirical research might substantiate the fact that the greater portion of potential investors does not rely on prospectuses for information before making an investment decision. More fundamentally, research might disprove or at least weaken the case for the prophylactic worth of SEC mandatory disclosure. In such a case, enactment of a regulation which requires issuers to prepare and register prospectuses with the SEC would be seriously questionable from any standpoint. Although a few investors might be assisted by the information contained in the prospectus, it is doubtful that the benefits would outweigh the enormous costs of the regulatory system. In any event, this is information which should be known before the decision is made. Yet nowhere in this process is the validity of the initial assumption examined.

Serious scientific research, as it is understood in other disciplines,[4] is not a common pursuit of the legal profession.

Lawyers, law professors, and judges are trained to engage in language analysis and precedent gathering and have a natural reluctance to undertake systematic scientific research. This contributes significantly to the fact that much of securities law is based upon myth. While the myths may in fact be true, it is unlikely that the legal profession will be able to make this determination by using traditional legal methods. Even if the results produced by a particular law are questioned in order to determine if another law would be more beneficial, the answers usually are based upon intuition rather than on empirical studies.[5] The legal profession tends to ignore empirical issues. Yet if the legal profession is to make significant contributions to the development of legal rules, it is imperative that offices and law books be abandoned for research and examination of real-world data. This will involve the painful effort of learning new techniques, but the effort is essential in order to achieve desired societal goals in the regulation of securities transactions.[6]

Practitioners perhaps can be forgiven for assuming the empirical validity of corporate and securities law, or ignoring the problem altogether. Their professional preoccupation is to parse the words of statutes, divine the intent of judicial pronouncements, and guide their clients through the legal maze. The practitioners' primary concern must be to keep their clients free and clear of the legal bramble bush.

The academic legal profession is another matter. Their *raison d'être* should be to examine and probe the underlying empirical basis of the law in a scholarly and scientific manner. Unfortunately, law professors seldom address themselves to the empirical aspects of legal issues.[7] Instead, academicians concentrate on the production of articles that are too often word analyses and that frequently involve some form of the consistency approach.[8] Policy content is eschewed in the pursuit of doctrinal consistency.

Such writing often addresses important matters and should not be flippantly dismissed. Clarity of language is important in the law. Unfortunately, the truly important questions are frequently ignored. Do current broker/dealer registration requirements accomplish their goals or would an alternative regulatory scheme produce better results? Serious scientific research in the manner pursued by other disciplines could provide major insights into such questions, but to date this sort of research has been used far too little in the area of securities law.

This criticism is intended as a plea that lawyers in policymaking positions and law professors make a reasonable attempt to verify their hypotheses and decisions by empirical research whenever possible. This will involve not only the painful effort of learning the techniques of other social science disciplines, but also a significant increase in interdisciplinary research among lawyers, economists, social psychologists, and others in the field of corporate and securities law.

The basic thesis of this chapter can be illustrated by focusing on one of the major "bread and butter" legal issues in securities law: the private offering exemption. Analysis of the private offering exemption will demonstrate the current lack of empirical knowledge, the kinds of research that should be undertaken, and the fruitful results which might be achieved.

The Private Offering Exemption: A Test Case

Section 5 of the Securities Act of 1933[9] is the key provision regulating new issues of corporate securities. In essence, it prohibits the use of the mails or other facilities of interstate commerce to sell or offer to sell a security unless a registration statement (including a prospectus) has been declared effective by the SEC. The prospectus is the basic disclosure document which is sent to offerees and buyers of securities in a public offering. Preparation of the document requires the expert assistance of expensive attorneys, accountants, investment brokers, and financial advisers. The cost also includes the loss of productive time of corporate management and the cost of delay occasioned by the waiting time at the SEC.

The great expenses and long delays of Section 5 requirements have created a special burden on small corporations. The costs of going public the first time have increased dramatically over the years. Those costs have their most severe impact on relatively small issuers and small financings since the percentage of expenses incurred to capital raised by a public offering is higher for smaller financings.[10] The explanation is simple. Among the largest direct components of expenses are legal and accounting fees. Legal and accounting problems created by SEC regulation are frequently as complex for the smaller issuer as for the larger. It takes a great deal of skill and time to transform a closely held corporation into an entity that meets the legal and accounting demands of the SEC. Furthermore, the underwriting costs of small issuances are relatively higher than the costs of large issuances. The risks are also greater for the smaller corporation; one of the components of the risk is the legislatively created civil liability exposure. Time is another burden since SEC registration involves long delays and smaller issuers are less able than large corporations to deal with delay.

In response to the complexities and delays of the SEC registration process, counsel to small as well as large issuers have sought exemptive routes. For decades the principal routes were the private[11] and intrastate offering exemptions,[12] and the Regulation A conditional exemption.[13] The latter provided little support to small issuers since business and accounting data requirements, although less comprehensive than for a full registration statement, were still very burdensome. Another route was the intrastate exemption.[14] This exemption was designed to permit local financing, conducted entirely within one state. Unfortunately, it has been very technically construed both by the SEC and the courts and is a potential minefield for attorney and client.[15] Furthermore, this federal exemption does not exempt the issuer from state disclosure requirements that can be as onerous as federal requirements. The third exemption often used was the private offering exemption.[16] Successful compliance with this exemption would free the issuer from federal registration requirements and often from state disclosure filing requirements as well.

The leading case interpreting the private offering exemption is *SEC* v. *Ralston Purina Co.*,[17] involving a sale of nearly $2 million of unregistered stock to over 1000 employees of Ralston Purina. The test for exemption provided by the Supreme Court required the issuer to prove that the offerees had access to information and/or could "fend for themselves."[18] Since the basic purpose of the 1933 Act is to prevent fraud and to promote knowledgeable investing in the securities market through disclosure,[19] the *Ralston Purina* test serves in the case of private offerings as a substitute for the requirement of prospectus registration as a means of disclosure and prevention of fraud.

Commentators could never agree on the factors that would satisfy the *Ralston Purina* test (hereinafter referred to as the "judicial doctrine"). It was argued that exemption of a "private offering'' from the registration requirements of section 5 required either purchaser wealth and/or financial savvy. How much savvy or wealth was never satisfactorily fixed. Proof that the offerees had access to adequate information was also required. But how much information?[20] Some combination of some or all of these factors was thought to satisfy the definition of private offering under section 4(2).

In addition to the foregoing uncertainties in the doctrine, there were other perplexities. Many practitioners assumed that the number of offerees was a significant factor in obtaining an exemption. No one knew what the magic number was. The favorite number was twenty-five offerees, but at least where the offerees were institutions, that number could be exceeded with some impunity.[21]

The previously described variations and permutations of judicial doctrine do not necessarily have any coherent relationship to the original goal of the private offering exemption, which was to permit businesses to find viable alternatives to the SEC registration route within the spirit of the 1933 Act when raising capital. The intent of the doctrine is to balance the goal of investor knowledge against the goal of easy capital formation. The exemption could be limited to the deans of three leading business schools, but perfect knowledge or sophistication would be achieved at the expense of zero capital formation in registrationless private offerings. In defining the exent of the private offering exemption, the law should seek an optimal level of sophistication and of information disclosure. Different requirements of disclosure or sophistication may have real-world effects on capital formation. It is assumed that each of the various verbalizations of the private offering exemption result in different numbers of eligible investors, which further results in varying levels of capital formation. But, to date, the links in this chain remain in large part mere assumptions.

The linguistic varieties of the judicial doctrine are attempts to promote knowledgeable private offering investment. But those linguistic variations are meaningless if the impact of each change on real-world capital formation is unknown. How much capital formation is facilitated by what judicial doctrine? Such data are essential to intelligent doctrine formation. Neither the SEC nor the judiciary can weigh even roughly the benefits of one doctrinal shift against another without knowing both sides of the balance.

Two Cheers for Regulation D

The SEC attempted to ease the burden on financings. After more than forty years of confused regulation, the agency finally promulgated a safe harbor—Rule 146.[22] Unfortunately, the rule retained the prior elusive concepts of knowledge, access, and sophistication. It is unnecessary to repeat the voluminous literature exposing the fatal defects of this rule.[23] In 1980 the SEC made another effort to solve part of the problem by adopting Rule 242,[24] which permitted sales of up to $2 million of securities every six months to thirty-five individuals and an unlimited number of institutions. The Rule 146 requirements of sophistication were eliminated.

The SEC in 1982 made yet another series of changes with reference to small financing. Rules 146 and 242 as well as certain other regulations were abrogated. The SEC adopted in their place Regulation D,[25] exempting certain offerings from registration under Section 5 of the Securities Act of 1933. The new exemptions are more liberal in scope than their predecessors and, as such, they are to be welcomed. In their final form, however, they contain a fair number of arbitrary and almost humorous classifications and categories which defy rational explanation. In essence, they demonstrate that the Commission, in its retreat from the excesses of mandatory disclosure, can no longer fashion a rational exemptive structure.

New Rule 504 provides a complete SEC registration exemption and permits general solicitation and freedom of resale, as long as the offering does not exceed $500,000 and is registered in states that require delivery of a disclosure document.[26] The main principle of Regulation D is apparent. State mandatory disclosure protection is deemed fully sufficient for public offerings of that relatively small dollar magnitude, no matter how large the number of individual investors.[27]

There is, of course, no adequate empirical basis for the $500,000 cutoff. It is a completely arbitrary figure. Moreover, there is no floor or ceiling for adequate state disclosure. The state disclosure document can be short or long, trifling or unbearably persnickety; it does not matter. The exemption thus demonstrates the fragile nature of the federal mandatory disclosure system. The Commission has decided that mandatory federal disclosure is sufficiently unimportant to cut it off for offerings at the $500,000 level. Presumably that is a significant cutoff. That is, many thousands of investors and hundreds of deals will be exempt. (If it is not a significant cutoff, then the exemption is unimportant and not worth discussing.)

I further presume that the SEC believes that the states will assure that investors in under $500,000 public deals will not be stung despite the absence of a federal prospectus. However, why will they be stung in bigger public deals? If state disclosure is adequate, why stop at $500,000? Why not move up to $3 million or $4 million? There is no principled reason for not moving up. The SEC has set an arbitrary limit to its jurisdiction. It will not be able to stop erosion. The figure will move up over the years, but oh so slowly and painfully!

Next we move to Rule 505. That rule permits nonregistered offerings in amounts of $5 million over a twelve-month period to thirty-five naive, ignorant buyers plus an unlimited number of specified types of affluent or sophisticated purchasers who are called "accredited" purchasers in the rule. The magic number thirty-five was obtained from the American Law Institute's proposed Federal Securities Code, which, in turn, arrived at the number in the following manner, as described by the principal draftsperson, Loss:

> After we reached the point of saying a limited offering is an offering that results in not more than "X" buyers, we had to decide what should be the "X". Naturally, I started with twenty-five because that was more or less the rule at one time. Then, at one of the meetings of the advisory group, several of the Advisors said twenty-five might be a bit tight in some instances, because, after all, today you can rationalize an offering to more than twenty-five even without institutions. At that point, Commissioner Loomis, one of the Advisors, said: "I think I might take thirty-five," and I said: "sold"—and that is how we got the thirty-five.[28]

The numbering thirty-five is now embodied, perhaps forever, in regulatory cement. Up to thirty-five financial dummies can be stung. However, stinging thirty-six dupes will not be tolerated.

The thirty-five financial innocents, however, must receive a detailed financial and business disclosure package. The package is similar to that required by a full registration, although somewhat less detailed. Thank heavens at least for that difference! Therefore, Rule 505 is not really an exemption from mandatory disclosure. It is a qualified exemption that relieves the issuer of an SEC prospectur filing requirement. The Commission, however, in Regulation D, reserves the right to demand to see the financial and business disclosure package.

The reason for Rule 505 mandatory disclosure is mystifying. The thirty-five investors, we repeat, need not be financially sophisticated. Indeed, that is one of the chief goodies of Rule 505: the issuer need not seek out thirty-five qualified buyers. Yet those financially ignorant innocents must be given a complex disclosure package, which presumably they cannot understand.

No disclosure is specified when the Rule 505 offering is made only to accredited purchasers. This is small comfort to the corporate issuers of stock. Accredited purchasers include institutions such as insurance companies. They did and will continue to get more disclosure out of the issuer than 1000 SEC regulations could ever produce. Other accredited persons are individuals with net worths above $1 million, or, for example, individuals with incomes in excess of $200,000. These individuals were usually well able to take care of themselves in the past and did not need a Regulation D to help them. However, the SEC is, in a way, a consumer protection agency for the affluent and this rule illustrates it. It eases the regulatory path for offerings to institutions and the wealthy. Granted, the path was already smooth; now it will be somewhat smoother. This is helpful to the extent it facilitates capital formation. However, whether the difference will be material is problematical.

Next we move to Rule 506. Unlike Rule 505, the offering amount is unlimited. The trade-off is that the thirty-five nonaccredited purchasers must be sophisticated (alone or with a representative). However, in the SEC lexicon there is sophistication and there is *sophistication.* Accredited purchasers are deemed to be sophisticated under the rule and hence need not (if they are the only buyers) be furnished with specified information. Presumably, they will demand what is appropriate. The nonaccredited sophisticated investor, however, must be supplied with specified information similar to that required in a full registration, although in somewhat less detail. Presumably, he is sophisticated but somehow still naive enough to need government assistance. For example, his net worth may be $600,000, not $1 million, or he may be that puzzling personality, a financially astute yet penniless character. Of course, the accredited wealthy individual (e.g., net worth of more than $1 million) may be a financial nitwit but still she is presumed by the Commission not to be so.

As in the past, the buyer in a fully registered deal can indeed be a financial nitwit. There is no bar to that. In the 506 deal, he or she cannot be such. This embodies the principle that large groups of buyers in registered deals can be financial ignoramuses, no regulatory problem; but small groups of nonaccredited buyers in 506 deals must be sophisticated. True, the buyer in a registered deal can use Section 11 of the 1933 Act. The buyer in an exempt deal must use Rule 10b-5 or Section 12(2) but that is a relatively small matter on which to rest so large a distinction.

Regulation D is better than the old structure since the old structure was absolutely terrible. But it is not a brave new world. The bar is happy with this rule and the rest of Regulation D, of course. Their clients get more than they did under the prior rules. Thus Regulation D demonstrates that if the past is bad enough, some improvement will bring forth huzzahs.

CONCLUSION

Very basic investigations must be made to establish just what is happening in the real world of private offerings (or any other piece of securities regulation). The following are the kinds of information that must be gathered.

1. What differing judicial theories of law are lawyers actually using?
2. Do differing theories result in varying frequencies of aborted deals, in differences in amounts of capital raised, or in different classes of offerees?
3. How successful are investments in private transactions?
4. Is there any relationship between such success and the legal theory used?
5. What are the differences between the handling of private offerings prior to and subsequent to promulgation of a rule, such as Rule 146 or Regulation D, in terms of capital raised, time to complete the deal, fees, or success of the investment?

The need for this research can be illustrated further by contemplating possible responses to the research.

1. Investigation may show that differing judicial theories have no differential impact upon the level of sophistication of the purchasers or the amount of capital raised. On the other hand, a differential impact may be identified that will demonstrate the value of one theory over another.
2. Investigation may demonstrate that capital raising is just as difficult, more difficult, or less difficult, after the promulgation of Rule 146 (or Regulation D) than it was before.
3. Research may show that in certain kinds of transactions, the judicial doctrine, however verbalized, has no relation to practice. Thus the typical private financing of a small or medium-sized corporation may violate the convention legal theories most of the time.
4. Some findings may vary depending upon the region of the country, size of the law firm, experience of the lawyer, or nature of the business that is raising capital.

Law professors who write about various exemptions from SEC registration requirements know none of the answers to the foregoing questions. For example, in talking to various practitioners I frequently get the impression that there is an incalculable gap between the judicial doctrine as understood by the SEC and that perceived by private attorneys. This may be due to great differences in legal interpretation of the correct doctrine, ignorance of the doctrine, or the impossibility in reality of structuring deals in conformity with the doctrine. Ignorance of what is actually occurring in private offerings makes legal scholarship in this area nonsense.

Research will enable lawyers to formulate private offering theories that actually make possible more knowledgeable investing while minimally hampering the goal of capital formation. Moreover, if the research shows that differences in theory have no impact on knowledgeable capital creation, law professors and SEC regulators can stop spending endless hours on theoretical nonsense and move on to more rewarding endeavors.

Certain arguments may be raised against the use of empirical research in examining these questions, such as cost, the difficulty of utilizing reliable methods of research, and determining whether empirically valid answers will be obtained. Nevertheless, significant research has been conducted in areas of comparable complexity and sensitivity. Questionnaires and interviews frequently can be used with considerable success. For example, interviewing methods have been used to develop data on the sensitive area of directorial behavior in the governance of corporations.[29] There is a vast body of this kind of research in the social sciences. Of course, there is a cost to research, but without such endeavors, law professors are limited to sterile and secondarily important verbal scholarship.

An enormous amount of securities law involves naive empirical assumptions: naive not because they are necessarily false, but because they are seldom validated empirically. Legal contributions too often are limited to word analysis of SEC and judicial regulations. Every second-year law student can parse the prose of a judicial opinion; any law professor can present a helpful synthesis of the law in a given area. Both are helpful as far as they go. But if law professors limit themselves to that level of analysis they are doomed to the pursuit of the relatively trivial.

The questions crying out for empirical research are legion. These questions occasionally are posed at the SEC, in judicial opinions, and in scholarly articles. But they are presented in a conventional legal mode of analysis which structurally is remote from reality. It is as if corporate and securities law bears the same relation to reality as Aristotelian science to the modern scientific method. Lawyers cogitate and speculate in an ethereal void, free from empirical feedback.

The SEC in very recent years has retained some sophisticated new economic staff and is improving its efforts in these matters. The SEC general staff, however, is still attorney-dominated and disposed to produce more regulations than even a hardy small band of economists can evaluate effectively.

The conventional response of legal academicians to such questions is benign neglect. When the empirical results of current doctrines are questioned, too often the response is silence. Legal scholars and practitioners involved in law reform efforts must pursue these issues in empirical terms if they are to deserve a reputation for serious scholarship.

15

SEC Regulation
of Attorneys

IN RECENT YEARS the Securities and Exchange Commission has not limited itself to corporate disclosure regulation. It has attempted to force the private bar to become an auxiliary enforcement arm of the SEC staff attorneys. In this regard the interests of the private and the public bar have diverged. This is to be expected. Both SEC staff attorneys and the private bar have a common interest in more regulation. The SEC staff, however, has a particular interest in controlling the private bar since that will increase its own power and responsibility.

SEC PHILOSOPHY REGARDING
ATTORNEY CONDUCT

During the entire decade of the 1970s and at least until the inauguration of the Reagan administration, the SEC was engaged in a vigorous campaign in the courts and administrative proceedings to turn corporate attorneys away from their historic role as advocates and advisers of clients and into independent legal auditors of corporate conduct.[1] The SEC has two platforms from which it launches actions against attorneys. The first is an injunction action.[2] In such proceedings the SEC attempts to convince a federal district court that the attorney has culpably furnished erroneous legal advice to corporate officers or directors which furthers or abets violation of securities laws by such corporate officials. The SEC's second and more potent weapon against attorneys, however, has been the controversial Rule 2(e).[3] That rule of conduct was promulgated by the SEC and gives, or purports to give, the agency power to discipline lawyers and accountants or disbar them from SEC practice. According to one of the standards set forth in that rule, the SEC can proceed against an attorney who has violated appropriate professional standards. Pursuant to a second criterion in that rule, the SEC can proceed against attorneys who have willfully violated or willfully aided and abetted violation of SEC rules or regulations.[4] The rule as interpreted by the SEC applies to the entire scope of securities practice.[5] It is not limited to attorney misbehavior while arguing a case before the SEC in its adjudicatory function. Thus it covers legal advice given in the attorneys' office. Many securities attorneys question the authority of the SEC to promulgate or implement the rule. Indeed a recent SEC Commissioner, Roberta Karmel, frequently dissented from Rule 2(e) proceedings against attorneys.[6] She vigorously questioned the SEC's legislative authority to promulgate the rule in its current far-reaching form.[7] Furthermore, she persuasively argued that the SEC disbarment power dampens the private bar's zeal in representing the clients before the SEC since the agency has enforcement as well as quasi-judicial powers over them and their clients.[8]

The number of Rule 2(e) proceedings has been on the increase. Karmel has pointed out that "although Rule 2(e) has been in effect in some form since 1935, the Commission did not bring its first disciplinary proceedings against an attorney until 1950.[9] An insignificant total of only five cases were begun before 1960.[10] Astoundingly, however, as Karmel pointed out, "during the past decade . . . the Commission embarked upon a program for improving professional responsibility which resulted in the institution of over 85 cases against attorneys since 1970.[11] Either attorneys were remarkably irresponsible in the last decade or the SEC was up to a fairly disturbing attempt to coerce and intimidate the bar.

The SEC has prosecutorial power to bring injunctive actions in the federal district courts and administrative proceedings before administrative law judges; it also has discretion to make criminal references to the Justice Department. The SEC uses those powers to enforce the questionable financial and business disclosure rules previously discussed in this book. For many years the agency has taken the position that the securities attorney is the foundation of the disclosure system. There is some truth to this, in that attorneys play an important role in advising corporations on disclosure obligations and the concepts of materiality. The SEC has reached out beyond this rather banal observation, however, to use Rule 2(e) to control and mold the conduct and nature of private legal advice. As Karmel points out:

> A primary rationale for so using Rule 2(e) has been that "the task of enforcing the securities laws rests in overwhelming measure on the bar's shoulders" and that given "its small staff, limited resources, and onerous tasks the Commission is peculiarly dependent on the probity and diligence of the professionals who practice before it." However, Congress did not authorize the Commission to conscript attorneys to enforce their clients' responsibilities under the federal securities laws.[12]

In proceeding down this dangerous path the SEC hopes to accomplish two purposes: First, to force corporate attorneys to tilt their legal advice in the direction and mode demanded by the SEC, and second, to chill the adversarial instincts of the bar. For example, assume that Attorney Amy Brown, the general counsel of the publicly held XYZ Corporation, learns that the corporation has failed to disclose a new material contract. The company's chief executive officer explains to her that he has what he thinks is a good business reason to delay disclosure temporarily. The current doctrine permits at least temporary suppression of the news if valid business purposes justify it, especially if rumors of the news have not permeated the market.[13] The SEC perhaps may interpret the judicial doctrines more severely than the private bar. In her initial thinking, Attorney Brown believes that the chief executive officer's business judgment is reasonable. If she decides that there is no disclosure violation and the SEC subsequently disagrees with her, however, she runs the risk of being disbarred from SEC practice by the SEC. If she counsels the corporation to disclose her risks are minimal. She will continue to hold her job and will not run the risk of disbarment. If her corporate officer colleagues complain about her response, she will be able to point to the SEC bias toward disclosure to justify her decision. Timid lawyers will always be powerfully impelled to follow what they imagine will be in the views of the SEC. Even their less timid colleagues will find it in their self-interest to follow the path of their more risk-averse legal colleagues.

In the recent Carter and Johnson case the SEC for the first time in many years moved in a more healthy direction.[14] In dismissing an action against two attorneys, the SEC strictly construed the aiding and abetting component of Rule 2(e) as requiring some element of knowingly aiding the wrongdoer on the part of the attorney.[15] Next, it adopted a fairly pragmatic and flexible approach to an attorney's professional and ethical responsibility to report to the board of directors an officer's refusals to heed the attorney's legal advice.[16] The SEC, however, asserted its right to articulate in the future the professional and ethical standards of securities attorneys in their practices, and, of course, reiterated its support of the legality of Rule 2(e) and its powers under that rule.[17] These two factors constitute a continuing threat to the independence of the securities bar. Although there is now some hope that in future Rule 2(e) proceedings the SEC will be more sensitive to the need for an independent bar, that dream is subject to the unfettered discretion of the SEC. Despite the fact that a recent general counsel, Edward Greene (under a new, more conservative SEC), in January, 1982 recommended that the SEC take a more modest role in disciplining attorneys,[18] I venture to predict that the Carter and Johnson opinion, in spite of its "acquittal" of the two attorneys will, because of its continuing reservation of Rule 2(e) powers to the SEC, prove in the long run to be of little solace to attorneys. The SEC will, I predict, continue to wage its decade-long campaign to restructure the role of attorneys and change them from advocates into arms of the state. The SEC simply has too many incentives to curb and control the bar for anyone to trust its future "benevolent despotic" reticence.

ATTORNEYS AS AUDITORS OF CORPORATE CONDUCT

Historically, the attorney in American society has been the adviser to and advocate of the interests of his client. He is the individual or institutional client's right hand, sword, and shield in time of conflict, and trusted counselor at all times. In his professional capacity he must subject his interests to those of the client. Much of our freedom under law in Western society is dependent upon the legal professional's fulfillment of these historic functions. The SEC in its ten-year long campaign to change the behavior of the legal profession has attempted to revolutionize this historic structure and turn the attorney into an independent auditor of corporate conduct. Under this philosophy, the profession would become the indirect enforcement arm of the state and federal governments.

CONSEQUENCES OF SEC LITIGATION

The side effects of this evolving new structure have been, and I predict will be, serious and adverse. To begin with, corporate officers and employees will no longer be able to trust and use the corporate general counsel's office or outside counsel to the same degree as in the past. They would be foolish to do so, in many cases, since corporate attorneys acting under fear of Rule 2(e) proceedings will be quick to disclose their confidences to higher-ups in the corporation or even to expose them to the public. Wise corporate management and employees will increase the scope of decisions made without benefit of legal counsel.

Attorneys will act increasingly as auxiliaries of state and federal governments. They will assume an oversight role beyond that ever envisaged for outside directors and more similar to the role of government-appointed directors of the corporation. Their ultimate responsibility, under the SEC approach, would be to the enforcement arm of government agencies, not to the corporation of its shareholders. It is difficult indeed to distinguish between attorneys in this new role, and the concept of government directors. Many critics of the American corporation have called for legislation to place government-appointed individuals on corporate boards. The purpose of a government director of a corporation would be to *police* corporate activity in the light of existing judicial and statutory law. This is the identical purpose of the legal profession under the SEC philosophy. A similar role is being forced upon the independent accounting profession by SEC litigation in the courts during the past ten years. Unlike attorneys, however, accountants are intended to be auditors, not advocates.

There is far too much government regulation in our society.

One of the remaining barriers between the private individual or institution and an overreaching government is a vigorous legal profession. The profession can fulfill that role only by taking a position of challenge to government. That is the value of the requirement that the legal profession zealously defend and represent the interests of its clients. Unfortunately, the SEC has been vigorously attempting to change the relationship of the lawyer to the corporate client. Spokesmen of the SEC enforcement division have on many occasions candidly expressed the opinion that private attorneys have a duty similar to that of SEC attorneys to endorse the securities laws.[19] The limited enforcement staff of the SEC would thus be supplemented by the energies of thousands of private practitioners. That is, I submit, an extremely dangerous philosophy. Although we can hope that Carter and Johnson's move to a more modest SEC role in disciplining attorneys represents an end to the decade-long SEC campaign against lawyers, we will not be able to feel secure until the legislature or the Supreme Court strips the SEC of its overly expansive Rule 2(e) authority.

PART VI

Corporations and Public Policy

16

Corporations as Mediating Structures

TRADITIONAL VIEWS OF THE CORPORATION

In the preceding sections of the book I have established a theory of the existence and functioning of the corporation. I have, I believe, demonstrated the weaknesses of the traditional view of the corporation.

As we now know, the conventional philosophy pictures the publicly held corporation as a kind of ministate. Hence the creation of duties of loyalty and care and the support given to independent directors and SEC surveillance as a method for curbing the arbitrary use of corporate power. The economic view espoused by this book has pointed out the power of the markets for control and the inadequacies of the traditional modes of governmental regulation.

The traditional approach, however, is seriously deficient in a deeper and more fundamental sense. It pays attention to the bones, but ignores the muscle and flesh. By its emphasis on a governmental analogy, the traditional philosophy actually lays the seeds for its own destruction. Let us dwell on this point, for it will illustrate the fatal defect of the conventional approach while at the same time indicating the relationship between the economic mode and the morality of the corporation.

Democratic governments, needless to say, derive their authority from the consent of the governed. The democratic process succeeds when officials are elected by a fair and open system. Fundamental to this process is the "one person, one vote" concept. There are grave flaws in the system as it operates but, as we are fond of saying, none better has yet been devised.

If the publicly held corporation is erroneously viewed as a kind of ministate, however, then the present system of corporate governance is not only flawed, it is hopelessly false. To begin with, the system is based upon "one share, one vote," not "one person, one vote." Hence the traditional mode of looking at the corporation has at its very center an impossible conundrum. The corporation viewed as a polity is obviously not a Jeffersonian model of democracy. As I pointed out in Chapter 8, suggestions have been made to magnify the power of the small individual shareholder. But as I also demonstrated, that method will destroy the economic efficacy of the corporation in that it will drive out the large investors.

PROPOSED SOLUTIONS OF TRADITIONALISTS

The other traditional solutions to the problem of corporate accountability to stockholders and the public are hopeless palliatives. The move to make independent directors the dominant force on corporate boards is absurd. If the corporation is not subject to effective competitive restraints by the marketplace, then who can place any faith in a small group of nondemocratically elected independent directors from the business world? The American public will not for long place much hope or credence in them.

Another approach is to place so-called constituency directors on the board. These would include representatives of various women's and minority groups. But as I have previously demonstrated, these groups would have their own agendas. They would not have a business agenda. They would not be primarily concerned with corporate success or shareholder interests. Therefore, placing these directors on the board would widen, not narrow, the gap between shareholders and management.

Another hopeless palliative is the attempt to charge the corporation with the nebulous goal of "social responsibility."[1] This means that corporations should strive to maximize "societal" or "communal" values rather than maximize profits.[2] Any adequate definition must realize, as Manne has so aptly put it, that *"corporate social expenditure or activity [are those] . . . for which the marginal returns to the corporation are less than the returns available from some alternative expenditure.* [Emphasis added.]"[3] If we take away this fundamental axiom, we are left with nothing but *"Adam Smith's unseen hand, which by virtue of selfish individual behavior, guides all economic resources to their socially optimal use.* [Emphasis added.]"[4]

Examples of corporate social expenditures include neighborhood rehabilitation. If neighborhood rehabilitation by a corporation would pay off in enhanced business profits, then Adam Smith and everyone else would advocate corporate rehabilitation of the neighborhood. If it would not increase profits, indeed if it would lower profits or cause a loss, then the corporation that rehabilitates would be engaging in a corporate social expenditure.

Now that we have defined corporate social expenditures accurately, two crucial weaknesses in the usual corporate social-responsibility argument emerge. First, there is precious little room in competitive industries for significant "social expenditures." Those corporations that pay for "good works" will at their own peril benefit their competitors who concentrate on profit maximization. This point is illustrated by the parable of six competing corporations, each with plants on the same river. All of them are polluting the stream, and assume that no federal or state statutes require antipollutant devices. One of the corporations *voluntarily* decides to build a costly new pollution-free factory. Thereupon its costs rise and it is forced to charge a higher price for its product. The five "bad guy" corporations continue to pollute the stream with their low-cost, refuse-spreading plants. As a necessary consequence of the brute facts of competition, the five "bad" corporations drive the "good" corporation out of business, to the gain of the stockholders of the five "bad" corporations, but to the great economic loss of the thousands of shareholders and employees of the "good" corporation. Incidentally, many of these employees and shareholders may no longer be able to afford college tuition for their children. That is a social loss, I assume, as well as an economic loss to society. Meanwhile the river stays polluted. Apparent corporate social responsibility has conflicted with corporate profit maximization and has been socially impotent as well. The effective solution is responsible governmental action, such as an antipollution tax policy, not corporate voluntary action.

A second crucial weakness is that the apparently felicitous phrase "corporate social responsibility" masks the fatally ambiguous nature of the concept. One man's "social responsibility" is another man's social poison. For example, in the 1960s Dow Chemical Company sold napalm to the U.S. Defense establishment for use in the Vietnamese war. Shareholders attempted to get the policy changed by use of the shareholder-proxy and annual-meeting machinery.[5] The court disclosed that

> [t]he decision to continue manufacturing and marketing napalm was made not *because* of business considerations but *in spite* of them; that management in essence decided to pursue a course of activity which generated little for the shareholders and actively impaired the company's public relations and recruitment activities because management considered this action morally and politically desirable.[6]

The point is that if we free up corporate management so that corporations can pursue political and other nonbusiness ends, some of us may abhor the end results. The proponents of corporate social responsibility cannot effectively deal with the fact that corporate involvement in "social" activity means that, for better or worse, corporate officers will determine our social goals. For example, Henry Ford, in an effort to make a profit, established new modes of mass production. This benefited society. He also directed his efforts at his "social" goals: he financed anti-Semitic acts. Is it not dangerous to permit corporate management to use corporate resources to accomplish their own "social" aims?[7] I do not mean by this that corporations should not continue to make responsible contributions to charitable and educational institutions. I simply wish to emphasize the danger of going too far in the direction of transforming corporations into social as distinguished from business institutions.

In conclusion, the notion of corporate social responsibility is dangerous because it would give too much power to corporate big shots to determine our social goals. Top corporate management should limit themselves to the purely economic role of maximizing profits within the confines of law and generally accepted ethical behavior. Government should be used to accomplish societal goals, not private corporations.

The judicially created notions of duty of care and duty of loyalty are not without value. They are fundamentally and inevitably vague in content, however, and seem a weak basis, indeed, on which to rest the legitimacy of the government of the mega-corporation.

In the final analysis the debate over governance turns on how best to control corporate management. The traditional theory I have analyzed in this book has at best developed a series of pitiful palliatives: independent directors, audit committees, duty of loyalty, and SEC regulation.

The alternative philosophy espoused in this book is fundamentally a truer and better approach to the legitimacy issue. It emphasizes the *value* to the shareholders of the split between ownership and control. It demonstrates the *disciplining value* of the markets for management and control. It reveals the inadequacies of SEC regulation and the excessive costs of such regulation.

THE CORPORATION AS MEDIATING STRUCTURE

There is another crucial factor that adds to the relevance and strength of the economic arguments presented in this book. The American corporation acts as a vital mediating structure between the powerful state and the individual.[8] Our democratic capitalist system permits, indeed facilitates, so-called mediating structures between the state and the individual. These entities include the family, the community organizations, churches and synagogues, and the modern publicly held corporation.

The corporation is not a unique institution in American society. There are many nongovernmental organizations with size and power, including trade unions, churches, and huge foundations. Consider the Roman Catholic Church, an immensely influential organization that is organized along nondemocratic lines. Its membership has no input into the selection of priests, bishops, and cardinals. In communist countries, the power of the church is recognized to the point that the communist party attempts to control the church apparatus directly. The conflict between church and state in Poland is but one example.

Foundations are another example. The small groups that control the Ford, Getty, or similar foundations have tremendous influence on the American cultural and economic scene. Again, in totalitarian societies the state eliminates such nonstatist organizations.

The family is another mediating influence. It stands between the state and the individuals in critical areas of personality development and maturation.

The importance of the mediating function of the corporation to the democratic free enterprise state is also crucial. If government were to seize control over the corporation, then the free enterprise society would largely vanish and be replaced by a form of socialism. At that point the autonomy of economic man would have ended. Government would make all the significant economic decisions.

In short the modern corporation is the method by which men and women are free to make *economic* decisions without state control. Just as the autonomy of religious institutions allows us to pursue spiritual activity free of state control, and foundations permit freedom from government control in cultural affairs, and just as the university permits freedom from state control in the intellectual domain, so the corporation permits freedom in the economic kingdom.

The church may arouse the ire of its members. Likewise a university may follow an intellectual policy that enrages an individual teacher or group of professors. There is no individualistic nirvana that will satisfy each and all at the same time. This is not a valid argument, however, for placing church and university under state control. Indeed on this point there is fairly universal consensus in the American society. The same consensus does not exist for the corporation. In large measure this is because of the fact observed elsewhere by Schumpeter[9] and others that academicians and church leaders distrust the business elites. The freedom they demand for themselves they do not extend to the business leadership.

Of course, it may be argued that the large corporation may oppress some shareholders or certain employees or communities. Hence the assumed need for government control over the board of directors or the senior management. But we have dealt with that issue in prior sections of the book. We have, I believe, demonstrated that the legal controls are frequently at best inefficient. On the other hand we have demonstrated the impressive disciplining effects of the capital markets to curb management and at the same time permit the average small shareholder to leave the enterprise whenever he pleases.

The traditional theory of the corporation found in big business boardrooms, the SEC, and the books of corporate law professors has no intellectual justification. In all fairness it does not hold a candle to the radical critique of the corporation. The SEC and the corporate bar would have you believe that corporations are powerful entities possessing great power over hundreds of thousands of employees and shareholders, which power is successfully circumscribed by groups of middle-aged independent directors who are largely corporate executives and by the mandatory disclosure requirements of the SEC statutes. In reality, this is not a theory but a series of prayerful palliatives. If I thought that was the best the corporate community could do in the way of philosophy, I would turn them over to the tender mercies of Ralph Nader tomorrow.

Shareholders of the corporation have placed capital with managers. The managers coordinate the input of capital (and labor) subject to the powerful forces of the market that were described in Chapter 5. Shareholders are not subject to some totalitarian corporate dominion. They are free, as we have pointed out, to sell whenever they perceive management inefficiency and dishonesty.

The managers have power. Their power, however, has been greatly exaggerated in the popular press. As Novak recently pointed out:

> Examining the Fortune 500 at ten-year intervals shows that even large corporations are subject to the cycle: new ones keep appearing and many that were once prominent disappear. Of the original Fortune 500, first listed in 1954, only 285 remained in 1974.[11]

The largest corporations are subject to the vigors of the marketplace. Chrysler will fail unless it again begins to satisfy the consumer. Even General Motors and Ford will decline or fail unless they meet the competition of the Japanese auto industry. These forces plus the market for control and management produce corporate vigor and efficiency.

Even Karl Marx recognized the productive genius of free enterprise; and after decades of experience with socialist command economies, some radicals are beginning to concede the necessity for market approaches. At the center of free market productivity is the modern publicly held corporation. Without it there is no alternative but the wasteful and totalitarian command economy model.

The vigor of corporate enterprise depends upon the separation of the corporation from the government. Just as we have demonstrated that separation of ownership and control is not some original sin, separation of corporations from the government is not a flaw but is in fact essential to the continued existence of the modern democratic capitalist state.

The necessary autonomy of the publicly held mega-corporation does not mean that the republic is helpless to accomplish certain collective results. We are all familiar with the expressions "market failure" or "externalities." This now-popularized economic jargon refers to certain transactions that are not disciplined by the marketplace. Pollution is a popular example. Corporations that pollute do not have to pay the cost of the pollution, hence they produce more of it than is socially acceptable. Society, through the federal Congress or state legislatures, can control corporate pollution activity by tax policy or direct regulation. This is not the place to argue which is the better approach or how often market failures occur, or how often they can be controlled by laws which facilitate more effective free-market approaches. The point is that society can in limited but significant areas control corporate decisions by legislation or taxation. I say limited because obviously excessive regulation and control will destroy the productive capacities of the corporation.

The corporate model has certain costs. There is no doubt that managers of the corporation are not popularly elected officials. The SEC can promote as many independent directors as it has the power to create, it can proliferate audit committees and proxy rules until the agency is blue in its governmental face; the fact will remain that business managers will run their businesses short of total government ownership or control. The traditional philosophy criticized in this book does not work. The economic model embraced in this work explains the operation of describing market forces in a realistic manner. There are costs; managers may exercise power in nonbeneficial ways, but those occasions will be far fewer than imagined by the critics of the corporation.

17

The Entrepreneurial Corporation and Its Enemies: Concluding Remarks

THE GREAT BULK OF SEC and corporate law is based upon a fear of the split between absentee passive shareholders and the managers, termed the separation of ownership and control.[1] Since the managers are in power and the shareholders are scattered and passive, the courts and the legislature have developed various legal doctrines that surround managers with ambiguous legal restrictions couched in terms of "fairness" and "overreaching" and "waste" and the like.[2] Hence also the SEC and the corporate bar have developed the traditional model of the corporation as a static quasi-government in need of constant regulatory surveillance. Indeed, corporate law as it has developed and matured is consumed by an obsessive fear of conflict of interest and a belief in the ability of law to solve it. Brilliant indviduals devote their lives to legal careers in which they largely waste their talents devising contracts and litigation to curb the supposedly malevolent forces of management. Squads of equally talented at-

Material in this chapter is taken with changes from Nicholas Wolfson, "SEC Thinking About Corporate Governance and Accountability: Lessons in Bureaucratizing the Entrepreneurial Corporation," in *Corporate Governance: Past and Future*, p. 5 middle through most of p. 8. Copyright © 1982 by KCG Productions, Inc. Reprinted by permission.

torneys spend their time defending corporations from such litigation or devising modes of behavior that will lessen the likelihood of
such suits.

The principal effect of SEC and corporate law is to
bureaucratize the corporation, entangle it in litigation, and
dampen the entrepreneurial spirit. In fact, the movement for independent directors and stiffer legal duty of care requirements
can be understood as a device to minimize the power of manager-
entrepreneurs in the corporation by placing them under the
supervision of risk-averse quasi-bureaucrats, called outside or independent directors, who will be preoccupied with safety, regulation, and the past, rather than risk-taking and the future.

Lost in the maze of regulation is the truth that corporations
are efficient modes for organizing production and attracting
capital into the firm. Shareholders who have no interest or ability
to manage, willingly entrust their capital to management experts
who have the know-how and skill to organize production and earn
a return for the shareholders.[3] The overemphasis on the conflict of
interest between owner and manager creates a false problem since
their very separation is an indispensable method of organizing
production and entrepreneurial ability. The past growth and success of the modern American corporation is the key to American
productivity and that growth was made possible by the very split
between ownership and control that is troubling the SEC. That is
not to say, of course, that managers never slack off or commit
crimes or behave unfairly toward the shareholders. No one, including myself, is enough of a Pollyanna to hold that naive view of
the corporation. The point is, however, that even for the large
corporation, the competitive pressures of the marketplace act far
more swiftly and efficiently than regulation to marry the interest
of manager and shareholder.

All American corporations, operate in a fiercely competitive
economy that swiftly punishes a failure to satisfy the consumer.
The American automobile industry is painfully learning that
lesson today.[4] Management perishes when it does not produce
competitive products and succeeds when it does. The shareholder
benefits when management is successful and suffers when it is not.
There may be a lag—that is to say, lazy or inept management
may continue in power for a period of time while the shareholders
suffer—but it would be folly to believe that government regulators, part-time outside directors, or lawsuits based upon state

duty of care concepts can succeed where management has failed. Indeed, the problem with large American corporations is that they are not sufficiently entrepreneurial and aggressive. As Gilder has pointed out, large corporations tend to become too "rigid and specialized" and leave the innovative and technological break-throughs to the smaller new corporate entrepreneurs.[5] Needless to say, none of those smaller businesses owe their success to part-time outside directors or audit committees. Unfortunately, the heavy hand of SEC regulation on large corporations increases such tendencies toward rigidity. The essence of capitalism is risk-taking; the most striking characteristic of the businessperson is faith in the future and in the creative nature of his or her efforts. According to Johnson, "the successful entrepreneur is driven not so much by greed as by the desire to create. He has more in com-mon with the artist than the bureaucrat."[6] As Posner has pointed out, "because the individual cannot prosper in a market economy without understanding and appealing to the needs and wants of others, and because the cultivation of altruism promotes the effec-tive operation of markets, the market economy . . . also fosters empathy and benevolence, yet without destroying individual-ity."[7] Sadly, SEC staff attorneys and many other skeptics or critics of the free enterprise system are more comfortable with government administration than with capitalism. Even people in business tend to be apologetic about capitalism and to accept timidly the conventional fallacies of the SEC and the leftish reformers.

Essentially, shareholders and management are embarked to-gether in a creative venture that ideally is designed to benefit both of them as well as the public. In addition to the impact of product competition, compensation packages geared to profits provide an incentive for managers to perform well. Successful managers become wealthy. More important, they earn psychic rewards as their reputations grow.[8] Failures look for jobs outside of business. If management slacks off, shareholders sell out and buy into more efficient concerns.[9] The price of the stock drops, sending a power-ful message to management which knows that hungry and am-bitious takeover groups are lurking on the sidelines, ready to seize control from lazy or inefficient management.[10] The competitive incentives to work hard and produce for the benefit of the shareholders are enormous. Yet corporate law reformers, the SEC staff, Naderites, and the like continue to manifest a peculiar hostility to the American corporation and the business profession. As Gilder has observed, "hatred of producers of wealth still flourishes and has become, in fact, the racism of the intelligentsia."[11] In the halls of the SEC, in academia, and among some congressmen a continual war is being waged against the corporation and people in business. Hence the continual preoccupation of the SEC with corporate criminality and the venality of the corporation. Hence the continual pressure by the SEC and the academic reformers for changes in corporate governance and for increased SEC regulation. The bottom line of the reformers is to curb the power of management and place it in other hands. Their dislike of business is doubly ironic since it occurs at a time when the American economy needs all the entrepreneurial energy and risk-taking it can muster.

Notes

CHAPTER 1

1. A. Berle and G. Means, *The Modern Corporation and Private Property,* 1932.
2. M. Eisenberg, *The Structure of the Corporation,* 1976.
3. Berle and Means, op. cit.
4. See, e.g., W. Cary and M. Eisenberg, *Cases and Materials on Corporations,* 5th ed., 1980, pp. 140–149.
5. Ibid.
6. See e.g., Del. Code Ann. tit. 8, § 141(a) (1982).
7. See e.g., M. Mace, *Directors: Myth and Reality,* 1971.
8. See e.g., Sinclair Oil Corp. v. Levien, 280 A.2d 717 (Del. 1971).
9. See e.g., Shlensky v. Wrigley, 95 Ill. App. 2d 173 (1968).
10. Model Business Corporation Act § 35 (1979); see "Report of Committee on Corporate Laws: Changes in the Model Business Corporation Act," 30 *Business Lawyer* 501, 506 (1975).
11. See e.g., E. Veasey and W. Manning, "Codified Standard—Safe Harbor or Uncharted Reef? An Analysis of the Model Act Standard of Care Compared with Delaware Law," 35 *Business Lawyer* 919 (1980); S. Arsht and J. Hinsey, "Codified Standard—Same Harbor but Charted Channel: A Response," 35 *Business Lawyer* 947 (1980).

12. See e.g., Zahn v. Transamerica Corp., 162 F.2d 36 (3d Cir. 1947).

13. See e.g., Del. Code Ann. tit. 8, § 144 (1982).

14. J. Bishop, "Sitting Ducks and Decoy Ducks: New Trends in the Indemnification of Corporate Directors and Officers," 77 *Yale Law Journal* 1078, 1079 (1968).

15. Securities Act of 1933, 15 U.S.C. §§ 77a–77aa (1976).

16. Securities Exchange Act of 1934, 15 U.S.C. §§ 78a–78kk (1976).

17. See e.g., H. Kripke, *The SEC and Corporate Disclosure: Regulation in Search of a Purpose,* 1979.

CHAPTER 2

1. A. Berle and G. Means, *The Modern Corporation and Private Property,* 1932, p. 94.

2. Ibid., p. 47.

3. Ibid., pp. 86–87 (footnote omitted).

4. Ibid., p. 87.

5. Ibid., p. 89.

6. Ibid., p. 121.

7. Ibid., p. 122.

8. Ibid., p. 122.

9. Ibid., p. 124.

10. Ibid., p. 278.

11. Ibid., pp. 340–341 (footnote omitted).

12. Adam Smith, *An Inquiry into the Nature and Causes of the Wealth of Nations,* p. 700 (E. Cannan ed., 1966).

13. Berle and Means, op. cit., p. 349.

14. Ibid., p. 351.

15. Ibid., p. 349.

16. Ibid., 337.

17. Ibid., pp. 355–356.

18. Ibid., p. 356.

19. Ibid., p. 159.

20. Ibid., p. 157 (footnote omitted).

21. Ibid., p. 308.

22. Ibid., p. 308.

23. Ibid., p. 308.

24. Ibid., p. 313.

25. Ibid., p. 313.

26. Ibid., p. 319.

27. Ibid., p. 319.

28. Ibid., p. 321.

29. Ibid., p. 287.

30. Ibid., p. 286.

31. Ibid., p. 357.

32. Ibid., p. 356.

CHAPTER 3

1. See e.g., Securities and Exchange Commission, Staff Report on Corporate Accountability, 96th Cong., 2d sess., Sept. 4, 1980, Committee Print (submitted to Senate Committee on Banking Housing and Urban Affairs) (hereinafter cited as SEC Report).

2. See e.g., R. Nader, M. Green, and J. Seligman, *Taming The Giant Corporation,* 1976; and J. K. Galbraith, *The New Industrial State,* 1967.

3. M. Mace, *Directors: Myth and Reality,* 1971.

4. See R. Townsend, *Up The Organization,* 1970, p. 49.

5. See e.g., Committee on Corporate Laws, "The Overview Committees on The Board of Directors (rev. ed.), 35 *Business Lawyer* 1335 (1980); "A.B.A. Corporate Director's Guidebook (rev. ed.)," 33 *Business Lawyer* 1591 (1978); N. Leach and R. Mundheim, "The Outside Director of the Publicly Held Corporation," 31 *Business Lawyer* 1799 (1976).

6. See address of Harold M. Williams, cited in H. Kripke, "The SEC, Corporate Governance and the Real Issues," 36 *Business Lawyer* 173, 178 (1981).

7. SEC Report, op. cit., pp. 496, 499, 500.

8. The New York Stock Exchange requires all domestically listed corporations to establish and maintain audit committees made up exclusively of independent directors. See "The Role and Composition of the Board of Directors of the Larger Publicly Owned Corporation, Statement of the Business Roundtable," 33 *Business Lawyer* 2083, 2109–110 (1978).

9. SEC Report, pp. 510, 515.

10. Ibid., p. 37.

11. D. Schwartz, "A Case for Federal Chartering of Corporations," 31 *Business Lawyer* 1125 (1976).

12. See F. A. Hayek, *The Mirage of Social Justice,* 1976.

13. See R. Nader, M. Green, and J. Seligman, *Taming the Giant Corporation,* 1976.

CHAPTER 4

1. R. Coase, "The Nature of The Firm," 4 *Economica* 386 (November 1937); reprinted in G. J. Stigler and K. E. Boulding, eds., *Readings in Price Theory,* 1952, p. 331.

2. Ibid., p. 332.

3. A. Alchian and H. Demsetz, "Production, Information Costs, and Economic Organization," 62 *American Economics Review* 777 (1972); reprinted in H. Manne, *The Economics of Legal Relationships: Readings in the Theory of Property Rights,* 1975, p. 555.

4. Coase, op. cit., p. 336.

5. Coase, op. cit., p. 337.

6. B. Klein, R. Crawford, and A. Alchian, "Vertical Integration, Appropriable Rents, and the Competitive Contracting Process," 21 *Journal of Law and Economics* 297 (1978).

7. Ibid., p. 308 (citation omitted). Messrs. Klein, Crawford, and Alchian recognized the earlier work on opportunistic behavior by Oliver Williamson and David J. Teece. See O. Williamson, *Markets and Hierarchies: Analysis and Antitrust Implications,* 1975, pp. 26–30; and D. Teece, *Vertical Integration and Divesture in the U.S. Oil Industry,* 1976, p. 31.

8. Klein, Crawford, and Alchian, op. cit., pp. 321–322 (citations omitted).

9. Alchian and Demsetz, op. cit., p. 777.

10. Ibid.

11. The concepts of "shirking" and monitoring are closely related to the economic theory of agency costs, and were developed by economics Professors A. Alchian and H. Demsetz. See Alchian and Demsetz, op. cit., p. 777. See also A. Alchian, "Corporate Management and Property Rights," in H. Manne, ed., *Economic Policy and the Regulation of Corporate Securities,* 1969, p. 337. For a survey of the recent literature in the fields covered by this section, see F. Furubotn and S. Pejovich, "Property Rights and Economic Theory: A Survey of Recent Literature," 10 *Journal of Economic Literature* 1137 (1972).

12. Alchian and Demsetz, op. cit., p. 777.

13. The cost to the organization of the agent's self-interest, in addition to the cost of detecting shirking, constitutes the agency costs of the enterprise. These costs include: (a) the cost of monitoring expenditures; (b) the cost of incentives to encourage the agent to work for the benefit of the organization; (c) so-called "bonding costs" of the agent which he may sometimes incur to convince the skeptical employer that he will indeed be loyal; and (d) a "residual loss" resulting from the selfish acts of the agent. See M. Jensen and W. Meckling, "Theory of the Firm: Managerial Behavior, Agency Costs and Ownership Structure," 3 *Journal of Financial Economics* 305, 308 (1976).

14. Ibid., p. 328.

15. S. Basu, "Investment Performance of Common Stocks in Relation to Their Price-Earnings Ratios: A Test of the Efficient Market Hypothesis," 32 *Journal of Finance* 663 (1977); P. Davies and M. Canes, "Stock Prices and the Publication of Second-Hand Information," 51 *Journal of Business* 43 (1978); W. Hillison, "Empirical Investigation of General Purchasing Power Adjustments on Earnings Per Share and the Movement of Security Prices," 17 *Journal of Accounting Research* 60 (1979); S. LeRoy, "Efficient Capital Markets: Comment," 31 *Journal of Finance* 139 (1976).

16. See generally P. Cootner, ed., *The Random Character of Stock Market Prices,* 1964.

17. Jensen and Meckling, op. cit., p. 305.

18. E. Fama, "Agency Problems and the Theory of the Firm," 88 *Journal of Political Economy* 288 (1980).

CHAPTER 5

1. See R. Posner, Economic Analysis of Law, 2d ed., 1977, pp. 300–05; A. Alchian and H. Demsetz, "Production, Information Costs, and Economic Organization," 62 *American Economic Review* 777 (1972). See also A. Alchian, "Corporate Management and Property Rights," in H. Manne, ed., *Economic Policy and the Regulation of Corporate Securities,* 1969 p. 337; M. Jensen and W. Meckling, "Theory of the Firm: Managerial Behavior, Agency Costs and Ownership Structure," 3 *Journal of Financial Economics* 305 (1976).

2. See generally P. Cootner, ed., *The Random Character of Stock Market Prices,* 1964.

3. See G. Benston, "The Costs and Benefits of Government-Required Disclosure: SEC and FTC Requirements: An Ap-

praisal," in D. DeMott, ed., *Corporations at the Crossroads: Governance and Reform,* 1980, pp. 37, 59.

4. H. Manne, "Mergers and the Market for Corporate Control," 73 *Journal of Political Economics* 110 (1965).

5. F. Easterbrook and D. Fischel, "The Proper Role of a Target's Management in Responding to a Tender Offer," 94 *Harvard Law Review* 1161, 1182 (1981).

6. Ibid., p. 1183.

7. Ibid., p. 1183.

8. Ibid., p. 1184.

9. Ibid., p. 1184, n.62.

10. Ibid., p. 1185.

11. Ibid., p. 1186 (footnotes omitted).

12. Ibid., p. 1186–88 (footnotes omitted).

13. M. Jensen, *Corporate Control: Folklore vs. Science,* Working Paper No. MERC 83-07, Graduate School of Management, University of Rochester (March 1983), pp. 6–7. See also M. Jensen and R. Ruback, "The Market for Corporate Control: The Scientific Evidence," 11 *Journal of Financial Economics* 5 (1983).

14. Jensen, *Corporate Control: Folklore vs. Science,* pp. 10–11.

15. E. Fama, "Agency Problems and the Theory of the Firm," 88 *Journal of Political Economics* 288 (1980).

16. W. Crain, T. Deaton and R. Tullison, "On the Survival of Corporate Executives," 43 *S. Econ. J.* 1372 (1977). See also W. Crain, "Can Corporate Executives Set Their Own Wages?" in M. Johnson, ed., *The Attack on Corporate America,* 1978, p. 272.

17. G. Stigler and C. Friedland, "The Literature of Economics: The Case of Berle and Means," 26(2) *Journal of Law and Economics* 237, 246 (1983).

18. Ibid., p. 249 (footnote omitted).

19. Ibid., pp. 249–252 (footnote omitted).

20. Ibid., p. 252.

21. Ibid., p. 254.

22. See generally G. Benston, "The Market for Public Accounting Services: Demand, Supply and Regulation" 2(1) *Accounting Journal* 2 (Winter 1979–1980). See also S. Ross, "Disclosure Regulation in Financial Markets: Implications of Modern Finance Theory and Signaling Theory," in F. Edwards, ed., *Issues in Financial Regulation,* 1979, p. 177.

23. In this regard, Professor George Benston has noted that prior to the passage of the Securities Act, most publicly held corporations whose

stock was traded on the New York Stock Exchange voluntarily retained certified public accountants and almost all firms released financial data to the public. "In 1926, 82 percent of the companies whose shares were traded on the New York Stock Exchange (NYSE) were audited by C.P.A.'s. By 1934 the percentage had increased to 94 percent." Benston, op. cit., pp. 37, 40 (note 7). "At least since 1926 all NYSE-traded corporations issued balance sheets and income statements." Ibid., note 8.

24. E. Herman, *Corporate Control, Corporate Power,* 1981, pp. 111–112.

25. Stigler and Friedland, op. cit., pp. 237, 254.

26. Ibid., pp. 254–258.

27. See P. Bohr, "Chrysler's Pie-in-the-Sky Plan for Survival," *Fortune,* 22 October 1979, p. 46; C. Burck, "A Comeback Decade for the American Car," *Fortune,* 2 June 1980, p. 52.

28. H. Demsetz, "The Structure of Ownership and the Theory of the Firm," 26 *Journal of Law and Economics* 375, 387 (1983).

29. Ibid., p. 388.

30. Ibid., p. 388.

31. Ibid., p. 389.

32. Ibid., p. 389.

33. Ibid., p. 389.

34. Ibid., p. 389 (referring to Wilbur G. Lewellen, "Management and Ownership in the Largest Firms," 24 *Journal of Finance* 299 [1969]).

35. Ibid., p. 390.

CHAPTER 6

1. "A.B.A. Corporate Director's Guidebook," 33 *Business Lawyer* 1591, 1600 (1978).

2. Securities and Exchange Commission, Staff Report on Corporate Accountability 96th Cong., 2d Sess., 4 September 1980, Committee Print (submitted to the Senate Comm. on Banking, Housing, and Urban Affairs), (hereinafter cited as SEC Report).

3. ABA-ALI Model Bus. Corp. Act, §35 (1979).

4. *Statement of the Business Roundtable on The American Law Institute's Proposed "Principles of Corporate Governance and Structure: Restatement and Recommendations,"* Feb. 1983, p. 48 (hereinafter cited as Roundtable).

5. 692 F. 2d 880 (2d Cir. 1982). This case involved the duty of care in the context of derivative suits. I examine this issue on page 89.

There I develop the argument that the Second Circuit misapplied its doctrine to the particular facts of that case.

6. Ibid., p. 885 (citations omitted).

7. Ibid., p. 886.

8. SEC Report, op. cit., p. 690. The SEC Report predated the *Joy* v. *North* Case, but the second Circuit's statement of the doctrine and its policy is at odds with the SEC staff philosophy.

9. Ibid., p. 690.

10. Ibid., p. 758.

11. The American Law Institute, *Principles of Corporate Governance and Structure: Restatement and Recommendations,* Tentative Draft No. 1 (April 1982), Part IV (hereinafter cited as ALI Principles). As this book was going to the printer, the ALI was issuing new tentative drafts. It is to be hoped that the final product will be more sensitive to the comments set forth in this chapter.

12. P. MacAvoy, "ALI Proposals for Increased Control of the Corporation by the Board of Directors: An Economic Analysis," in Roundtable, op. cit., p. C–22.

13. Roundtable, op. cit., pp. 39–51.

14. See ALI Principles, Part IV.

15. "Roundtable," op. cit., p. 50 (footnotes omitted).

16. See "Panel Discussion," 33 *Miami Law Review* 1519, 1545–46 (1979).

17. See Chapter 15.

18. In this regard, it must be emphasized that the duty of care discussed by the SEC Report, op. cit., pp. 657–91, operates when the directors do not have any conflict of interest that will interfere with the unfettered exercise of their business judgment.

CHAPTER 7

1. 33 *Business Lawyer* 1591 (1978).

2. Ibid., p. 1599.

3. Ibid., pp. 1599–1600.

4. Ibid., p. 1606.

5. Ibid., p. 1606.

6. See, e.g., Zahn v. Transamerica Corp., 162 F.2d 36 (3d Cir. 1947).

7. See generally W. Cary and M. Eisenberg, *Cases and Materials on Corporations,* 5th ed., 1980, pp. 550–693.

8. See, e.g., Pepper v. Litton, 308 U.S. 295, 306 (1939).

9. See, e.g., Rogers v. Hill, 289 U.S. 582 (1933).

10. Heller v. Boylan, 29 N.Y.S.2d 653, 679 (Sup. Ct. 1941) (Collins, J.), aff'd without opinion, 263 A.D. 815 (N.Y. App. Div. 1941).

11. See, e.g., T. Sowell, *Knowledge and Decisions* 1980, pp. 167–229.

12. See, e.g., W. Lewellen and E. Huntsman, "Managerial Pay and Corporate Performance," 60 *American Economic Review* 710 (1970); R. Masson, "Executive Motivation, Earnings, and Consequent Equity Performance," 79 *Journal of Political Economy* 1278 (1971).

13. W. Crain, "Can Corporate Executives Set Their Own Wages?" in M. Johnson, ed., *The Attack on Corporate America,* 1978, p. 277.

14. W. Crain, T. Deaton and R. Tollison, "On the Survival of Corporate Executives," 43 *Southern Economic Journal* 1372 (1977).

15. Ibid., p. 1372.

16. Ibid., p. 1372.

17. Ibid., p. 1374.

18. See generally V. Brudeny and M. Chirelstein, "A Restatement of Corporate Freezeouts," 87 *Yale Law Journal* 1354 (1978); "Note, Going Private," 84 *Yale Law Journal* 903 (1975).

19. See, e.g., Bryan v. Brock & Belvins Co. Inc., 490 F.2d 563, 570 (5th Cir.), cert. denied, 419 U.S. 844 (1974); "Note, Elimination of Minority Share Interest by Merger: A Dissent," 54 *Northwestern University Law Review* 629, 635 (1959).

20. M. Jensen and W. Meckling, "Theory of the Firm: Managerial Behavior, Agency Costs and Ownership Structure," 3 *Journal of Financial Economics* 305, 333 (1976).

21. A minimal legislative rule might be acceptable, to the effect that no going-private buy-out could be at less than a current market (e.g., last sale on exchange) price. For the reasons given in the reasons given in the text no other rule would be necessary.

22. See, e.g., Irving Trust Co. v. Deutsch, 73 F.2d 121 (2d Cir. 1934), cert. denied, 294 U.S. 708 (1935); Lincoln Stores Inc. v. Grant, 309 Mass. 417 (1941).

23. See Chapter 5.

24. See, e.g., Case v. New York Cent. R.R. Co., 15 N.Y.2d 150 (1965).

25. Sinclair Oil Corp. v. Levien, 280 A.2d 717 (Del. 1971).

26. A. Berle and G. Means, *The Modern Corporation and Private Property,* 1932, p. 244. For a sampling of the debate over the sale of control issue, see W. Andrews, "The Shareholders' Right to Equal Opportunity in the Sale of Shares," 78 *Harvard Law Review* 505 (1965).

27. 219 F.2d 173 (2d Cir.), cert denied, 349 U.S. 952 (1955).

28. Ibid., p. 178.

29. See, e.g., Thompson v. Hambrick, 508 S.W.2d 949, 954 (Tex. Civ. App. 1974).
30. See Chapter 13
31. See Chapter 5.

CHAPTER 8

1. See W. Cary and M. Eisenberg, *Cases and Materials on Corporations,* 5th ed., 1980, p. 141.
2. See E. Aranow and H. Einhorn, *Proxy Contests for Corporate Control* 2d ed., 1968, p. 363.
3. See Cary and Eisenberg, op. cit., p. 231.
4. Ibid., pp. 261–365.
5. Rosenfeld v. Fairchild Engine & Airplane Corp., 309 N.Y. 168 (1955).
6. Ibid.
7. R. Nader, M. Green, and J. Seligman, *Taming the Giant Corporation,* 1976, pp. 128–130.
8. See Chapter 5.
9. M. Dooley, "Should Management's Control of the Corporation Be Weakened, and That of the Shareholder Strengthened?" in M. Johnson, ed., *The Attack on Corporate America,* 1978, p. 84.
10. Nader, Green, and Seligman, op. cit., p. 130.
11. R. Winter, *Government and the Corporation,* 1978, p. 50.

CHAPTER 9

1. See e.g., Securities and Exchange Commission, *Staff Report on Corporate Accountability,* 96th Cong., 2d Sess., Sept. 4, 1980, Committee Print (submitted to the Senate Comm. on Banking, Housing and Urban Affairs), Chapter 6.
2. See, e.g., "Statement of the Business Roundtable: The Role and Composition of the Board of Directors of the Large Publicly Owned Corporation," 33 *Business Lawyer* 2083, 2109 (1978).
3. See H. Kripke, "The SEC, Corporate Governance, and the Real Issues," 36 *Business Lawyer* 173, 178 (1981).
4. See Sec. Exch. Act Rel. No. 18532 (3 March 1982).
5. For a critical discussion of various rival board philosophies, see K. Andrews, "Rigid Rules Will Not Make Good Boards," 60 *Harvard Business Review* 34 (November–December 1982).
6. Ibid., p. 39.

7. For the Investment Company Acts' requirements, see 15 USC § 80a-10.

8. See The New York Stock Exchange requirement in Listed Company Manual § 303.

9. P. MacAvoy, "ALI Proposals for Increased Control of the Corporation by the Board of Directors: An Economic Analysis," Feb. 1983, p. C-34.

10. Ibid., p. C-38.

11. Ibid., p. C-42.

12. See J. Letts, "Corporate Governance: A Different Slant," 35 *Business Lawyer* 1505, 1510 (1980).

13. SEC Report, op. cit., p. 559 (citing Heidrick and Struggles, Inc., *The Changing Board: Profile of The Board of Directors,* 1977, p. 11).

14. See generally H. Kripke, *The SEC and Corporate Disclosure: Regulation in Search of a Purpose,* 1979.

15. SEC Report, op. cit., p. 604.

16. See, e.g., 15 U.S.C. § 77aa (1976).

17. See G. Benston, "The Costs and Benefits of Government-Required Disclosure: SEC and FTC Requirements: An Appraisal," in D. DeMott, ed., *Corporations at the Crossroads: Governance and Reform,* 1980, pp. 37, 40 n.7.

18. R. Watts and J. Zimmerman, *The Markets for Independence and Independent Auditors,* Working Paper Series No. GPB 80-10, Graduate School of Management, University of Rochester, June 1981.

19. Auerbach v. Bennett, 47 N.Y.2d 619 (1979).

20. Joy v. North, 692 F. 2d 880 (2d Cir. 1982).

CHAPTER 10

1. Securities and Exchange Commission, *Staff Report on Corporate Accountability,* 96th Cong., 2d Sess., 4 September 1980, Committee Print (submitted to the Senate Comm. on Banking, Housing, and Urban Affairs, p. 496 (hereinafter cited as SEC Report).

2. Ibid., p. 499.

3. Ibid., p. 500.

4. Ibid., p. 502.

5. Ibid., p. 503 (quoting R. Mautz and F. Neumann, *Corporate Audit Committees: Policies and Practices,* 1977, p. 90).

6. Ibid., p. 486. The New York Stock Exchange requires all domestically listed corporations to establish and maintain audit committees comprised exclusively of independent directors. See "Statement of the Business Roundtable: The Role and Composi-

tion of the Board of Directors of the Larger Public Owned Corporation," 33 *Business Lawyer* 2083, 2109–110 (1978).

7. See, e.g., 15 U.S.C. § 77aa (1976).

8. See G. Benston, "Required Disclosure and the Stock Market: An Evaluation of the Securities Exchange Act of 1934," 63 *American Economic Review* 132, 133 (1973).

9. SEC Report, op. cit., pp. 498–99 (quoting E. Green and B. Falk, "The Audit Committee—A Measured Contribution to Corporate Governance: A Realistic Appraisal of Its Objectives and Functions," 34 *Business Lawyer* 1229, 1241 (1979).

10. See N. Wolfson, "The Need for Empirical Research in Securities Law," 49 *Southern California Law Review* 286 (1976).

11. R. Watts and J. Zimmerman, *The Markets for Independence and Independent Auditors,* Working Paper Series No. GPB 80–10, Graduate School of Management, University of Rochester, June 1981.

12. See text at note 14, Chapter 9.

13. G. Benston, "The cost and Benefits of Government-Required Disclosure: SEC and FTC requirements, An Appraisal" in D. DeMott, ed., *Corporations at the Crossroads: Governance and Reform,* 1980, pp. 37, 56.

14. SEC report, op. cit., p. 125.

15. Ibid., p. 528.

16. 17 C.F.R. § 240.14a–8 (1982). In August, 1983, Rule 14a–8 was amended. Sec. Exch. Act Rel. 20091 (August 16, 1983). The amendment will tighten eligibility by requiring a shareholder to own at least 1 percent or $1000 in market value of a corporation's securities before being permitted to submit a proposal. This is still a relatively small holding.

17. SEC Report at 37.

18. See N. Wolfson, "Securities Regulation," 1 *Corporation Law Review* 67 (1978).

19. SEC Report, op. cit., p. 510.

20. Ibid., p. 515.

21. Ibid., p. 514.

22. See, e.g., W. Cary and M. Eisenberg, *Cases and Materials on Corporations,* 5th ed., 1980, pp. 643–67.

CHAPTER 11

1. E. Furubotn, *The Economics of Industrial Democracy: An Analysis of Labor Participation in The Management of Private Business Firms,* Center for

Education and Research in Free Enterprise, Texas A & M University, Research Monograph No. 1 (June 1979), p. 9.

2. Ibid. See also E. Furubotn, The Economic Consequences of Codetermination on the Rates and Sources of Private Investment in S. Pejovich, ed., *The Codetermination Movement in the West: Labor Participation in the Management of Business Firms,* 1978, p. 131; E. Furubotn, "The Long-Run Analysis of the Labor Managed Firm: An Alternative Interpretation," *American Economic Review* 66 (March 1976): 104.

3. Furubotn, op. cit., p. 15.

4. As I explain later, it is unlikely that each labor group in each plant will select a different mix and that workers can then move from plant to plant selecting a mix. But if that were to happen, the system would then merely mimic today's system.

5. Furubotn, op. cit., p. 17.

CHAPTER 12

1. There is a considerable amount of discussion about what management methods or qualities will best accomplish such a process. But research as to the proper qualities necessary for senior management-bound success is only in its beginning stages. See generally K. Andrews, "Rigid Rules Will Not Make Good Boards," 60 *Harvard Business Review* 34 (November–December 1982).

CHAPTER 13

1. See Securities Exchange Act of 1934, ch. 404, tit. I, § 4, 48 Stat. 885 (1934) (current version at 15 U.S.C. § 78(d) [1981]). The Act was approved June 6, 1934. When the SEC was created in 1934, it also acquired responsibility for the enforcement of the Securities Act of 1933, 15 U.S.C. §§ 77aa–77aa (1981).

2. Each weekly issue of the Bureau of National Affairs (BNA) and Commerce Clearing House (CCH) securities advance sheets aggregates 75 to 100 printed pages of new administrative work product, illustrating that despite its age, the SEC retains significant regulatory force.

3. ALI Fed. Sec. Code (1980).

4. See generally L. Lowenfels, "The Case Against the Proposed Federal Securities Code," 65 *Virginia Law Review* 615 (1979). Lowenfels's article extensively and critically analyzes the changes

proposed in the Code and concludes that its enactment as a whole would be unjustified (ibid., p. 661). Lowenfels acknowledges the contributions of the framers of the proposed Code, but suggests that each individual provision be subjected to intensive legislative scrutiny before any changes in the present legislation governing securities are made (ibid., p. 661).

5. N. Wolfson, "Comments on the Proposed Federal Securities Code: Transformation of the Securities Act of 1933," 33 *University of Miami Law Review* 1495 (1979). For further discussion of the Code, see generally Symposium on Federal Securities Code," 33 *University of Miami Law Review* 1425 (1979).

6. Revised Interstate Commerce Act of 1978, Pub. L. No. 95–473, 92 Stat. 1337 (codified at 49 U.S.C. §§ 10101–11915 [1979]).

7. Airline Deregulation Act of 1978, Pub. L. No. 95–504, 92 Stat. 1705 (codified at 49 U.S.C. §§ 1301, 1302, 1305–1308 [1979]).

8. See P. Weaver, "Regulation, Social Policy, and Class Conflict," *The Public Interest,* No. 50, 45, 48 (Winter 1978).

9. Ibid., p. 48.

10. G. Stigler, "The Theory of Economic Regulation," in *The Citizen and the State: Essays on Regulation,* 1975, p. 114.

11. The genesis of the Interstate Commerce Commission is instructive. In the late nineteenth century, every hamlet of the United States was traversed by railroad lines. Competition over long-distance hauls was fierce. In the case of many short-distance hauls, however, customers frequently had the choice of only one railroad. Competition drove down long-distance railroad rates. Frequently, short-distance rates, for example from A to B to C to D, were greater than the rate from point A to point D. Customers complained and the railroad industry seized the opportunity to influence Congress to establish the Interstate Commerce Commission. The results were predictable. Long-distance rates went up and short-distance rates remained high; competition was chilled and existing carriers benefited. Thus, the effect of the establishment of the Interstate Commerce Commission, as is the case with many regulatory agencies, was to burden rather than benefit the rate-paying public. See M. and R. Friedman, *Free to Choose,* 1980, pp. 194–203. For examples of other research on the efficacy of regulation, see W. Wardell and L. Lasagna, *Regulation and Drug Development* (American Enterprise Institute for Public Policy Research, 1975); S. Peltzman, *Regulation of Pharmaceutical Innovation: The 1962 Amendments* (American Enterprise Institute for Public Policy Research, 1974); T. Moore, "The Beneficiaries of Trucking Regulations," 21 *Journal of Law and Economics* 327, 340 (1978).

12. See 15 U.S.C. § 2053 (1976).

13. Weaver, op. cit., p. 51.

14. See 42 U.S.C. § 4321 (1976).

15. Weaver, op. cit., p. 51.

16. See 29 U.S.C. §§ 651–678 (1976). Under the Occupational Safety and Health Act of 1970 (OSHA), Pub. L. No. 91–596, 84 Stat. 1590, the Occupational Safety and Health Review Commission was created to carry out "adjudicatory functions" necessary to OSHA, 29 U.S.C. § 651(b)(3) (1976). This Commission is granted authority pursuant to 29 U.S.C. § 661 (1982).

17. Weaver, op. cit., p. 51.

18. Ibid., p. 51.

19. See note 11, above.

20. See note 31, below.

21. See, e.g., Securities Exchange Act of 1934, §§ 10(b), 11(a)(2), 11(b), 14(a), 17(d)(1), 15 U.S.C. §§ 78j(b), 78k(a)(2), 78k(b), 78n(a), 78q(a) (1982).

22. Securities Exchange Act of 1934, § 6, 15 U.S.C. § 78f (1982).

23. Securities Exchange Act of 1934, § 15A, 15 U.S.C. § 78o–3 (1982). See generally N. Wolfson, R. Phillips, and T. Russo, *Regulation of Brokers, Dealers, and Securities Markets* (1977 and Supp. 1982), ch. 12.

24. Securities Exchange Act of 1934, § 19, 15 U.S.C. § 78s (1982).

25. Stigler has concluded in a study that by far, most SEC commissioners are either executives or lawyers. G. Stigler, "The Process of Economic Regulation," in *The Citizen and the State* (1975), pp. 145, 164–66.

    Stigler actually understated the importance of attorneys who have always dominated the activities of the agency. For example, in recent years a minimum of four out of the five Commissioners have been attorneys. Also, most of the important staff positions are always held by attorneys.

26. See generally P. Shuchman, *Problems of Knowledge in Legal Scholarship,* 1979.

27. See SEC Transition Team Final Report (22 December 1980), p. 65.

28. A. Berle, Jr. and G. Means, *The Modern Corporation and Private Property,* 1932.

29. See Medical Comm. for Human Rights v. SEC, 432 F.2d 659, 676 (D.C. Cir. 1970), vacated and remanded for dismissal as moot, 404 U.S. 403, 405 (1972). In Medical Committee for Human Rights, Dr. Quentin D. Young, National Chairman of the Medical Com-

mittee for Human Rights and a shareholder of Dow Chemical, requested on behalf of the committee that a resolution be presented to the shareholders of Dow Chemical to amend its charter (ibid., pp. 661–62). The resolution would have prevented the production of napalm (ibid., p. 663). Dow argued that under rule 14a-8, as then in effect, promulgated under § 14(a) of the Securities Exchange Act of 1934, 15 U.S.C. § 78(n)(a) (1970), shareholder proposals motivated by political or moral concerns or dealing with the conduct of the corporation's ordinary business operations were not required to be added to proxy proposals (ibid., p. 676). In its discussion of § 14(a), the court said: "It is obvious to the point of banality . . . that Congress intended by its enactment of section 14 of the Securites Exchange Act of 1934 to give true vitality to the concept of corporate democracy" (ibid., p. 676). The court cited legislative history of the Exchange Act which indicated that the legislation was drafted in part to correct the problem of the division of corporate ownership from management:

> But as management became divorced from ownership and came under the control of banking groups, men forgot that they were dealing with the savings of men and the making of profits became an impersonal thing. When men do not know the victims of their aggression they are not always conscious of their wrongs.

Ibid., p. 676 (quoting H. R. Rep. No. 1383, 73d Cong., 2d Sess. 5, 13 [1934]). According to the court, the legislative history indicated that the purpose of the Act was to force management to become more responsive to the needs and wishes of the corporation's owners.

30. According to the stated purposes of the Exchange Act, "transactions in securities . . . are affected with a national public interest which makes it necessary to provide for regulation and control of such transactions . . . in order to protect interstate commerce, . . . and to insure the maintenance of fair and honest markets in [securities transactions]." Securities Exchange Act of 1934, § 2, 15 U.S.C. § 78b (1976). To this end, the SEC was created. Ibid., § 4, 15 U.S.C. § 78d (1976).

31. The SEC is authorized to investigate violations of securities legislation as well as breaches of the rules of a national securities exchange or registered securities association by a member of such exchange or association. Ibid., § 21, 15 U.S.C. § 78u (1976). In addition, the SEC is empowered to hold hearings, ibid., § 22, 15 U.S.C. § 78v (1975); and to make rules and regulations under the various provisions of legislation regulating securities trading. See, e.g., ibid., § 23, 15 U.S.C. § 78w (1976) (rulemaking under Exchange Act);

Securities Act of 1933, § 19, 15 U.S.C. § 77s (1976) (rulemaking under Securities Act).

32. See D. Ratner, "The SEC: Portrait of the Agency as a Thirty-Seven Year Old," 45 *St. John's Law Review* 583 (1971).

33. For a more complete exposition see N. Wolfson, "A Critique of Corporate Law," 34 *University of Miami Law Review* 959 (1980).

34. G. Benston, "The Costs and Benefits of Government-Required Disclosure: SEC and FTC Requirements: An Appraisal," in D. DeMott, ed., *Corporations at the Crossroads: Governance and Reform*, 1980, 37, 54–55 (footnotes omitted).

35. Ibid., p. 55.

36. Ibid., p. 55 (footnotes omitted).

37. See J. Langbein and R. Posner, "Market Funds and Trust-Investment Law," *American Bar Foundation Research Journal* 1, 15 (1976).

38. A. Ehrbar, "Index Funds—An Idea Whose Time Has Come," *Fortune*, June 1976, pp. 144, 147.

39. Langbein and Posner, op. cit., pp. 14–18.

40. Ibid., p. 1.

41. Ibid.

42. Brief for SEC as Amicus Curiae, p. 7 (quoting Hanley v. SEC, 415 F.2d 589, 597 [2d Cir. 1969]) in case of Slade v. Shearson Hammill & Co., [1973–1974 Transfer Binder] Fed. Sec. L. Rep. (CCH) ¶94,329 (1974).

43. For a more complete exposition of this phenomenon, see N. Wolfson, Commentary on "The Market for Public Accounting Services: Demand, Supply and Regulation," 2 *Accounting Journal* 78 (Winter 1979–80).

44. 17 C.F.R. § 230.405 (1980).

45. 401 F.2d 833 (2d Cir. 1968) (en banc), cert. denied, 394 U.S. 976 (1969).

46. Ibid., p. 849 (quoting List v. Fashion Park, Inc., 340 F.2d 457, 462 (2d Cir.), cert. denied, 382 U.S. 811 (1965)). In Texas Gulf Sulphur, the SEC alleged that the defendants, who were officers, directors, employees, or relatives of officers, directors, and employees of Texas Gulf Sulphur (TGS), had purchased TGS stocks or calls on TGS stock on the basis of inside information concerning TGS drilling for copper ore (401 F.2d at 839–42, 844). This trading on inside information, as well as a misleading press release, formed the basis for an alleged violation of § 10(b) of the Securities Exchange Act of 1934, the Act's antifraud provision (ibid., p. 839).

The defendants who had traded on inside information were held liable, as were the defendants responsible for the misleading press release (ibid., p. 842–43).

47. Ibid., p. 849 (quoting List v. Fashion Park, Inc., 340 F.2d 457, 462 (2d Cir.), cert. denied, 382 U.S. 811 (1965)). According to the court: "Whether facts are material within Rule 10b–5 when the facts relate to a particular event and are undisclosed by those persons who are knowledgeable thereof will depend at any given time upon a balancing of both the indicated probability that the event will occur and the anticipated magnitude of the event in light of the totaling of the company activity" (401 F.2d at 849).

48. 426 U.S. 438 (1976). In Northway, a shareholder of TSC Industries, Inc. (TSC) alleged that a joint proxy statement that had been issued by TSC and National Industries, Inc., purchaser of 34 percent of TSC securities, was materially misleading (ibid., pp. 440–41. The Court stated that "materiality . . . is an objective [question], involving the significance of an omitted or misrepresented fact to a reasonable investor" (ibid., p. 445). The Court held that the representations and omissions by TSC and National were not materially misleading as a matter of law, and therefore reversed the court of appeals (ibid., pp. 452–53).

49. Ibid., p. 449. The Court pointed out in a footnote that its definition of materiality was supported by the SEC (ibid., n.10).

50. See, e.g., M. O'Connor and D. Collins, "Toward Establishing User-Oriented Materiality Standards," 138 *Journal of Accountancy* 67 (December 1974).

51. See, e.g., Financial Accounting Standards Board, *Discussion Memorandum, an Analysis of Issues Related to Criteria for Determining Materiality* (21 March 1975).

52. Indeed, a prestigious advisory committee's advice to the SEC is to avoid this quest for certainty and to continue consideration of materiality on a case-by-case basis as disclosure problems are identified. House Committee on Interstate & Foreign Commerce, Report of the Advisory Committee on Corporate Disclosure to the SEC, 95th Cong., 1st Sess., 3 November 1977, Comm. Print 95–29, p. 327.

53. 283 F. Supp. 643 (S.D.N.Y. 1968). Escott involved a class action suit by purchasers of 5.5 percent fifteen-year debentures against Barchris Construction Company. Plaintiffs brought suit under §11 of the Securities Act, alleging that the registration statement for the debentures had contained materially false and misleading statements and omissions (ibid., p. 652).

54. 1 S.E.C. 6, 8 (1934).

55. 283 F. Supp., p. 681.
56. Ibid., p. 682.
57. In recent years the SEC has established a unit called the Directorate of Economic and Policy Analysis. Its purpose is to conduct studies of SEC regulatory efficiency. Some of its studies, however, have already begun to have a practical impact. See e.g., Sec. Act. Rel. No. 6252 [1980 Transfer Binder] Fed. Sec. L. Rep. (CCH) ¶82675 (October 1980). The methods and purposes of the group are a model for the future of the SEC. Adequate methods must be developed to subject the ongoing regulatory process of the agency to sophisticated cost-benefit analysis and economic empirical research. An expansion of the Directorate is the correct approach to take and one that is recommended. At the same time, a significant slowdown in regulatory additions or changes must be instituted or the work of the Directorate will be similar in effect to King Canute's attempts to stop the ocean tide.

CHAPTER 14

1. Some observers have pointed to the need for empirical validation of the premises on which the securities laws are based. A notable example is Kripke, who has argued that a behavioral analysis of investors be undertaken to determine what information should be included in investment prospectuses. See H. Kripke, ''The SEC, The Accountants, Some Myths and Some Realities,'' 45 *New York University Law Review* 1151, 1175 (1970).
2. Section 5 of the Securities Act of 1933, 15 U.S.C. §77e (1976), in essence prohibits the use of the mails or other facilities of interstate commerce to sell or offer to sell a security unless a registration statement, including a prospectus, has been filed with the SEC. The prospectus is the basic disclosure document which is sent to offerees and buyers of securities in a public offering.
3. An example of this is a practitioner who, interpreting the Supreme Court's decision in SEC v. Ralston Purina Co., 346 U.S. 119 (1953), advises a client of the steps to take in order to insure that a private offering will qualify for exemption from registration.
4. There has been an active effort by economists and other social scientists to examine empirically the underpinnings of corporate and securities law. Frequently this work has led the way to important currents of change in the law. For example, the definitive study by Friend and Blume on the cost and profit structure of NYSE firms, demonstrating that small firms could survive competitive

commission rates, helped convince Congress to change the law which in the past had permitted fixed commission rates. See I. Friend and M. Blume, *The Consequences of Competitive Commissions on the New York Stock Exchange in Hearings on S. 3169 Before the Subcommittee on Securities of the Senate Committee on Banking, Housing and Urban Affairs,* 92d Cong., 2d Sess. (1972), pp. 259, 267–318.

5. For example, in an article on SEC Rule 144 governing the resale of securities issued in a private offering, the authors observed that "there is general agreement that it has been a major success in administrative rule making." M. Lipton, J. Fogelson and W. Warnken, "Rule 14—4-A Summary Review After Two Years," 29 *Business Lawyer* 1183 (1974). Many lawyers express the same viewpoints, but their conclusions are unconvincing without behavioral and other studies of the problem by trained investigators which will demonstrate how the rule is working.

6. Bayless A. Manning, former dean of Stanford Law School, once wrote that "the general field of corporation law has become hollow, empty, and largely devoid of policy content." Manning, "Discussion and Comments on Papers by Professor Demsetz and Professor Benston," in H. Manne, ed., *Economic Policy and the Regulation of Corporate Securities,* 1969, p. 81. As he so well put it, "corporation law has largely been flying by the seat of its pants, with little sense of target and *less data*" (ibid., p. 82, emphasis added). As Manning further points out: "Until we bring lawyer and social science disciplines together, we shall fall significantly short of being able to impart rationality into the process of ethics, bargaining and political assertion that we call lawmaking" (ibid., p. 87).

7. I once heard an eminent practitioner observe that law teachers too often write articles about matters which practitioners are better equipped to handle. For example, the legal literature abounds with articles on the scope of Rule 10b-5, the reach of Rule 144, and the latest twist in the definition of a security. Practitioners are on the firing line every day in these matters and know the bread-and-butter answers far better than academicians.

8. For example, a law review article might note that certain felony convictions within the prior ten years permit the SEC under the Securities Exchange Act of 1934 to refuse to register an applicant as a broker/dealer; yet another subsection of the 1934 Act permits the SEC to refuse registration to an applicant who has been enjoined from engaging in certain securities transactions even though that injunction was issued over ten years ago. Applying a consistency analysis, the author would suggest reform: to wit, insert the ten-year period in both sections or delete it from both. Thus, consistency is achieved. Another section of the article might analyze lan-

guage, point out terminological inconsistencies, and suggest clarification of the provisions regarding broker/dealers.

9. 15 U.S.C. §77e (1976).

10. G. Benston, "The Costs and Benefits of Government-Required Disclosure: SEC and FTC Requirements: An Appraisal," in D. DeMott, ed., *Corporations at the Crossroads: Governance and Reform,* 1980, pp. 37, 42.

11. Securities Act of 1933, §4(2), 15 U.S.C. §77d(2) (1976).

12. Ibid., §3(a)(11), 15 U.S.C. §77c(a)(11) (1976).

13. SEC Regulation A—General Exemptions, 17 C.F.R. §§ 230.251-.264 (1980).

14. Securities Act of 1933, §3(a)(11), 15 U.S.C. §77c(a)(11) (1976); SEC rule 147, 17 C.F.R. §230.147 (1980).

15. See Sec. Act. Rel. No. 4434 (6 December 1961).

16. Securities Act of 1933, §4(2), 15 U.S.C. §77d(2) (1976).

17. 346 U.S. 119 (1953).

18. Ibid., p. 125.

19. Securities Act of 1933, ch. 38, 48 Stat. 74 (preface).

20. In SEC v. Continental Tobacco Co., 463 F.2d 137 (5th Cir. 1972), the SEC in its brief took the onerous position that Ralston Purina required issuers to prove that each offeree had such a key relationship with the issuer that it gave him or her access to the corporate records and additionally to prove that each offeree was financially sophisticated. For a summary of the brief, see "Commission Stresses Burden of Proof Necessary to Support Use of Private Offering Exemption," 127 *Securities Regulation and Law Report* A-17 to A-18 (Nov. 17, 1971). The SEC staff and the courts have subsequently liberalized that position. See R. Jennings and H. Marsh, *Cases and Materials on Securities Regulation,* 5th ed., 1982, pp. 232–58.

21. A. Orrick, "Non-Public Offerings of Corporate Securities— Limitations on the Exemption Under the Federal Securities Act," 21 *University of Pittsburgh Law Review* 1, 10–11 (1959).

22. 17 C.F.R. §230.146 (1980).

23. See, e.g., M. Rosenfeld, "Rule 146 Leaves Private Offering Waters Still Muddied," 2 *Securities Regulation Law Journal* 195 (1974).

24. 17 C.F.R. §230.242 (1980).

25. See Sec. Act. Rel. No. 6389 (March 8, 1982).

26. When there is no delivery of a state disclosure document requirement, there is a bar on general solicitation and a restriction on resale.

27. Rule 504 requires that the issuer not be subject to the reporting requirements of Sections 13 or 15(d) of the 1934 Act.

28. L. Loss, "The 'Limited Offering' Under the American Law Institute's Federal Securities Code," in R. Mundheim, A. Fleischer, and J. Schupper, eds., *Fourth Annual Institute on Securities Regulation,* 1973, pp. 40–41.

29. E.g., M. Mace, *Directors: Myth and Reality,* 1971.

CHAPTER 15

1. See R. Karmel, *Regulation by Prosecution: The Securities and Exchange Commission versus Corporate America,* 1982, pp. 173–183 (hereinafter *Regulation by Prosecution*).

2. See e.g., Securities Exchange Act of 1934, § 21(d), 15 U.S.C. 78u(d) (1976); Attorneys and accountants may be found liable under §§ 5 and 17(a) of the Securities Act of 1933, 15 U.S.C. §§ 77e, 77q(a) (1976), as well as under § 10(b) of the Securities Exchange Act of 1934, 15 U.S.C. § 78j(b) (1976). See generally D. Ruder, "Multiple Defendants in Securities Fraud Cases: Aiding and Abetting, Conspiracy, in Pari Delicto, Indemnification, and Contribution," 120 *University of Pennsylvania Law Review* 597 (1972).

3. 17 C.F.R. 201.2(e) (1980). Rule 2(e) reads, in relevant part (with citations omitted):

(1) The Commission may deny, temporarily or permanently, the privilege of appearing or practicing before it in any way to any person who is found by the Commission after notice of and opportunity for hearing in the matter (i) not to possess the requisite qualifications to represent others or (ii) to be lacking in character or integrity or to have engaged in unethical or improper professional conduct, or (iii) to have willfully violated, or willfully aided and abetted the violation of any provision of the Federal securities laws . . . or the rules and regulations thereunder.

(2) Any attorney who has been suspended or disbarred by a Court of the United States or in any State, Territory, District, Commonwealth, or Possession, or any person whose license to practice as an accountant, engineer, or other expert has been revoked or suspended in any State, Territory, District, Commonwealth, or Possession, or any person who has been convicted of a felony, or of a misdemeanor involving moral turpitude, shall be forthwith suspended from appearing or practicing before the Commission. A disbarment, suspension, revocation or conviction within the meaning of this paragraph (e)(2) shall be deemed to have occurred when the disbarring, suspending, revoking or convicting agency or tribunal enters its judgment or order, regardless of whether appeal is

pending or could be taken, and includes a judgment or order on a plea of nolo contendere.

(3)(i) The Commission, with due regard to the public interest and without preliminary hearing, may by order temporarily suspend from appearing or practicing before it any attorney, accountant, engineer, or other professional or expert who, on or after July 1, 1971, has been by name:

(a) Permanently enjoined by any court of competent jurisdiction by reason of his misconduct in an action brought by the Commission from violation or aiding and abetting the violation of any provision of the Federal securities laws . . . or of the rules and regulations thereunder; or

(b) Found by any court of competent jurisdiction in an action brought by the Commission to which he is a party or found by this Commission is any administrative proceeding to which he is a party to have violated or aided and abetted the violation of any provision of the Federal securities laws . . . or the rules and regulations thereunder (unless the violation was found not to have been willful).

4. Id.

5. Regulation by Prosecution, p. 176.

6. In the Matter of Keating, Muething and Klekamp, [1979 Transfer Binder] Fed. Sec. L. Rep. (CCH) ¶ 82,124 (1979) at 81,992 (Karmel, Comm'r, dissenting).

7. Ibid., p. 81,992 (Karmel, Comm'r, dissenting).

8. Ibid., p. 81,992 (Karmel, Comm'r, dissenting).

9. Ibid., p. 81,994 (Karmel, Comm'r, dissenting) (footnotes omitted).

10. Ibid., p. 81,994 (Karmel, Comm'r, dissenting).

11. Ibid., p. 81,994 (Karmel, Comm'r, dissenting).

12. Ibid., p. 81,996 (Karmel, Comm'r, dissenting) (footnote omitted).

13. State Teachers Retirement Board v. Fluor Corp., 500 F. Supp. 278 (S.D.N.Y. 1980), aff'd in part, rev'd in part, and remanded, [1981 Transfer Binder] CCH Fed. Sec. L. Rep. ¶ 98,005 (2d Cir. 1981).

14. In the Matter of Carter and Johnson, [1981 Transfer Binder] Fed. Sec. L. Rep. (CCH) ¶ 82,847 (S.E.C. 1981). Commissioner Evans concurred with the dismissal of the charges against defendant Johnson but dissented from the dismissal of all charges that Carter aided and abetted the securities violations and rejected the majority's "method of articulating professional standards." Ibid., p. 84,173 (Evans, C., concurring in part and dissenting in part).

15. Ibid., pp. 84,166-67.

16. Ibid., pp. 84,169-73.

17. Ibid.

18. E. Greene, "Lawyer Disciplinary Proceedings before the Securities

and Exchange Commission, Remarks to the New York County Lawyers' Association,'' 14 *Securities Regulation and Law Report* 168 (20 January 1982).

19. See, e.g., S. Sporkin, ''What the SEC Expects from Corporation Lawyers,'' *Fortune* 23 October 1978, p. 143.

CHAPTER 16

1. D. Schwartz, ''Corporate Responsibility in the Age of Aquarius,'' 26 *Business Lawyer* 513, 515 (1970).

2. N. Jacoby, *Corporate Power and Social Responsibility: A Blueprint for the Future,* 1973, p. 197.

3. H. Manne and H. Wallich, *The Modern Corporation and Social Responsibility,* 1972, p. 4.

4. Ibid., p. 4.

5. *Medical Commission For Human Rights v. SEC,* 432 F.2d 659, 676 (D.C. Cir. 1970), vacated and remanded for dismissal as moot, 404 U.S. 403, 405 (1972).

6. Ibid., p. 681.

7. ''The 'Responsible' Corporation: Benefactor or Monopolist?,'' *Fortune,* November 1973, p. 56.

8. M. Novak, *The Spirit of Democratic Capitalism,* 1982; M. Novak and J. Cooper, eds., *The Corporation: A Theological Inquiry,* 1981.

9. J. Schumpeter, *Capitalism, Socialism and Democracy,* 1942.

10. See R. Coase, ''Advertising and Free Speech,'' 6 *Journal of Legal Studies* 1 (1977).

11. Novak and Cooper, op. cit., pp. 209–210 (footnote omitted).

CHAPTER 17

1. See A. Berle and G. Means, *The Modern Corporation and Private Property,* 1932; N. Wolfson, ''A Critique of Corporate Law,'' 34 *Miami Law Review* 959 (1980).

2. W. Cary and M. Eisenberg, *Cases and Materials on Corporations,* 5th ed., 1980, pp. 518–710.

3. See R. Posner, *Ecnomic Analysis of Law,* 2d ed., 1977, 289–314; A. Alchian and H. Demsetz, ''Production, Information Costs, and Economic Organization,'' 62 *American Economic Review* 777 (1972); M. Jensen and W. Meckling, ''Theory of the Firm: Managerial

Behavior, Agency Costs and Ownership Structure,'' 3 *Journal of Financial Economics* 305 (1976).

4. See P. Bohr, ''Chrysler's Pie-in-the-Sky Plan for Survival,'' *Fortune,* October 22 1979, p. 46; C. Burck, ''A Comeback Decade for the American Car,'' *Fortune,* 2 June 1980, p. 52.

5. G. Gilder, *Wealth and Poverty,* 1981, p. 77.

6. P. Johnson, ''George Gilder Praises Capitalism's Virtues,'' *Wall Street Journal,* 22 January 1981, p. 24.

7. R. Posner, ''Utilitarianism, Economics, and Legal Theory, 8 *Journal of Legal Studies* 103, 136 (1979).

8. See E. Fama, ''Agency Problems and the Theory of the Firm,'' 88 *Journal of Political Economy* 288 (1980).

9. See H. Manne, ''Mergers and the Market for Corporate Control,'' 73 *Journal of Political Economy* 110 (1965).

10. Ibid., p. 112.

11. Gilder, op. cit., p. 98.

Index